It Is Wonderful

Other Writings by Walter Lanyon

2 A. M. ◆ Abd Allah, Teacher, Healer
And It Was Told of a Certain Potter
Behold the Man ◆ Demonstration
Embers ◆ The Eyes of the Blind
The Impatient Dawn
Impressions of a Nomad
I Came ◆ It Is Wonderful
The Joy Bringer
The Laughter of God ◆ Leaves of the Tree
A Light Set upon a Hill
Life More Abundant
London Notes and Lectures
Out of the Clouds
Quintology: Ask and Ye Shall Receive
A Royal Diadem
The Temple Not Made with Hands
That Ye Might Have ◆ Thrust in the Sickle
Treatment ◆ Without the Smell of Fire
Your Heritage

Available through:
Mystics of the World
Eliot, Maine
www.mysticsoftheworld.com

It Is Wonderful

Walter C. Lanyon

It Is Wonderful

by Walter C. Lanyon

Mystics of the World First Edition 2017
Published by Mystics of the World
ISBN-13:978-1946362070
ISBN-10:1946362077

For information contact:

Mystics of the World
Eliot, Maine
www.mysticsoftheworld.com

Photography by © Dr. Joel Murphy 2017
www.DrJMphotography.zenfolio.com
Printed by CreateSpace
Available from:

Mystics of the World.com
Amazon.com

Table of Contents

Dedication

This book is dedicated to Father Divine[1], in appreciation for the glorious revelation his words brought to me. In my search for truth, I had met many wonderfully enlightened souls, noble and fine, some official stone casters, and a Judas. From all of these I received help and understanding. But it was not until I contacted Father Divine that I fully realized the Presence of the Power here and now. Not as something to be used to produce results, but as the very actuality of Being Itself.

After Jesus met Judas, he became fully conscious of the Christ.

It is with a heart full of love and thanksgiving that I dedicate this book to Father Divine, who has so richly given me of his Love.

Walter Clemow Lanyon

---

[1] All quoted italics in this book are words of Father Divine.

Note to the Reader

It came into expression as freely as the coming of dawn; a gift from the Region of the Unmanifest. For a few short weeks, I held it fluttering in the Soul of me and then released it. Like a golden mist, it enveloped me and finally poured out into manifestation as the soft dazzle of azure light on a silver mirror lake.

This is your book—a gift wherein is written a special message for you. It is a gift, and yet somehow you have consciously or unconsciously paid a price for it—the price of Love. It comes into your hands by divine direction. It is full of agreement and joy. It is redolent with light and healing. It has come to you for a purpose.

Blessings ... It is well.

Chapter I

Thou Art the Bright Messenger

Thou art the Bright Messenger—the Shining One, the being of pure Spirit. Thou art not the man thou hast been, lo these many years. Thou art newborn, fresh, clean, and pure. Thou art not an old creature patched up by various treatments. Thou, Bright Messenger, Golden One, hast never descended to the level of belief and therefore hast not consorted with the shadows of the play-life.

Thou art the Bright Messenger, with winged feet, who goeth where he will and knoweth no obstruction or condition. Thou art the unconditioned, the untrammeled, the free—the individualized yet inseparable manifestation of the All-God.

Thou art the Bright Messenger. Thou art full of light—bathed in All Light. Whithersoever thou goest is light—not consciously projected, but unconsciously conveyed; a natural effect of thy presence.

Thou art the Bright Messenger. Thine eye is single to the Allness of God, the Oneness of creation. Thou therefore seest with the eye of light. Thou lookest into a universe of All Light and seest through the shadows of belief. Thou seest the world in a world, the rose in a rose, and the Man in a man. Thou perceivest with thine eye of Light that which *is* and always has been—not that which shall be changed by begging, beseeching, or praying to a tyrant called God to make whole. With the eye of Light thou seest nothing to heal, for thy sight is perfect in the understanding:

"I am of too pure eyes to behold iniquity."

Thou art the Bright Messenger, the being of light. In the touch of thy hand is light. As the warmth of spring touches the frozen earth, so thy touch of light causes the seed to swell and burst and the flower to leap from her chalice. Thy touch of light is like the soft rain on the parched desert, which causes it to bloom as a rose. Whomsoever thou touchest—in the true sense of the word—thou transformest instantly, gloriously, freely, joyously. And men shall call it health, but thou shalt call it revelation.

Thou art the Bright Messenger. Thou hast the golden touch which transforms everything into the gold of which Ophir never dreamed. Thy touch shall be able to take from the fish's mouth the needed symbol. Thy touch it is which gives that which is beyond price and which makes a man rich, even when the saying goes "Silver and gold have I none; but such as I have give I thee." Such as thou hast in the touch, oh Bright Messenger, is beyond the price of pearls and rubies—the transforming touch which is gentle yet firm, which is soft like the surface of the ocean but has the power to dash a whole fleet of evil ships into oblivion. Thou art the Bright Messenger—thy touch is golden.

Thou art the Bright Messenger. The aroma of thy presence precedes thee. Thy passing is as the passing of a cloud of incense from the sacred lilies of the enchanted woods. In thy presence, the precious perfume of the soul is sensed above the stagnant odors of human beliefs. When thou comest to the soul, it is as the bridegroom before whom the lovely flowers of purity open and shed their perfume in superabundance. At thy coming, the rose loosens the silken tassel of her soul and gives forth the glorious attar of her being. At thy coming, the trees and minerals loosen the glorious, refreshing odors of woods and stones. From thy nostrils comes the Breath of Life. From thy breath comes the appearance of the new creation.

Man becomes a living soul by breathing thy breath—man lives and moves and breathes and has his being in thy breath. Thy breath fans the small sparks of faith into the flame of realization. From thy nostrils comes the flashing, dazzling fire which consumes the dross of belief. Thou art the Bright Messenger.

Thou art the Bright Messenger. Thy invitation is "O taste and see that the Lord is good." Eat my body (my substance) and drink my blood (inspiration). Thy taste is golden. The milk and honey of the universe of the All-God are thine. The hidden manna—that which the eye, the human belief, cannot see—thou feedest upon. Thy eternal drink is the Living Water. Thou shalt never be without the sustenance of Spirit, no matter whither thou goest. Thou shalt realize this all-substance and cease from thy thought-taking process of wondering wherewithal shall we be clothed and fed. Thou shalt eat, and hunger no more; drink, and thirst no more—for thou shalt feed upon the reality of life instead of the husks of material belief, with its shadow appearances.

Thou art the Bright Messenger, the bearer of glad tidings. Upon thy breastplate, encrusted in gold, is the motto "Speak no evil nor listen to." Thou art of too pure ears to hear evil—thou hearest with the ear of Spirit. Thou hearest with the silent ear, closed to the din of the human relative conditions but open to that which "eye hath not seen, ear hath not heard, neither hath it entered into the heart of man (human thought) the things which are prepared for them that love thy law." Thou hearest the word of peace, and a whole ocean of fury of belief ceaseth—stilled and made calm. Thou hearest the reports of that which *is*, and thou tellest of these. Thou hearest the things that ear hath not heard—the ear of man whose breath is in his nostrils and whose eye is double—and yet thou hearest the report of the Kingdom *here* and *now*; thou hearest the glad tidings of the eternal Christ walking today in the Garden of Attainment. Thou hearest the words "This is my beloved Son, in whom I am well pleased," and thou recognizest these words as addressed to thee.

Thou art not ashamed or afraid because of thy nakedness; the stark tragedies of the human belief fade into the distance when thou answerest this call with the "aye, aye" of Spirit. Thou hearest in the truest sense of the word, in the fearless sense of the word, "Arise and shine, for thy light hath come." No need to create this light, to stimulate it, but only to recognize this light as within.

How can a man who is constantly looking for evil to heal and treat know anything of the Kingdom? How can he understand the things which cannot be seen or heard with the human ears? How can he set right that which he has already done? And yet there are those poor deluded souls who have appointed themselves the official stone-casters for the Christ, not realizing that they are casting stones at him.

Thou art the Bright Messenger—the Being of Light—the unafraid. Why should there be fear when the realization has come that thou art the Bright Messenger, the being of pure Spirit, not subject to the beliefs of the thought-world, not subject to the failures and successes of thy human life, but suddenly up and above that which has always seemed so real.

Bright Messenger, Unafraid Being, Holy Creature, Son of God—arise, shine. Arise, let thy light so shine. Take no thought; if thou take thought, it will be of fear or limitation. Thou art the Bright Messenger, the Being of Light that goeth forth before the manifestation of thy human self and maketh straight the way. Thou art the Unafraid, the Unbound, the Prometheus Unbound. Thou shalt smite the rock and make it gush forth the Living Water of Life.

Thou art the Bright Messenger, the Being of Light, the Unafraid. Thou art glorious—thou art free—thou art not bound by human limitations. "Thou art not another (a separate one) but the same one." Thou art the Christ.

Hail! Soul of Me, I salute you, Son of God ... Christ ... Bright Messenger.

Chapter II

Assumption

He made himself as God ...
I and my Father are one.

It is natural that in making himself as God, becoming one with the Father, Christ partook quite freely of the divine nature. In other words, he *assumed* the nature of God. The demonstrations of a necessity followed—"the signs follow."

When man makes this *assumption*, when he recognizes that all life is God, he will *assume* the qualities of God naturally and find them out-pictured in his life. He will not then try to demonstrate the various attributes of this invisible Power but, by assumption, will be able to call them forth into manifestation at his will. "Ye shall decree a thing and it shall come to pass" can only be true of one possessing, or *assuming,* the God-nature. As long as this manifestation of God seems unusual or miraculous, just so long will it be little in evidence to him. But when man comes to the place where he "makes himself as God"— not *a* god but *as* God, of the same nature and substance— then by this assumption the natural flow of God-expression will take place, and he will begin to understand that he is "under grace."

He will understand and accept the truth of the statements "joint-heirs with Christ" and "Son of the living God." He will begin to make his *assumption* in the secret place within. He will recognize that, being created of God, he must of necessity partake of the nature of God. His assumption of his God-nature will have nothing to do with the former idea of wishing and hoping for things to come to pass. Once man is conscious of his true Self, his

14

decrees will be surrounded with confidence and abandon. He will not find it unnatural that the Son of the living God should appropriate the gifts of Spirit.

Assumption of the God-nature, as shown by the Master, is not akin to the old idea of visualization, wherein the person composed a picture to his liking and floated it in the imagination, trying to make it come into manifestation. Assuming the full "stature of Christ" is really contemplating the vision "shown you on the mount." You do not create it or imagine it. It is already existent and revealed to you. Assuming the divine nature (making yourself as God), man perceives the perfect where he formally saw the imperfect.

The Assumption of the Virgin (single-minded purity of consciousness) brought forth the new idea. The word became flesh—in other words, the assumption became manifest.

From the standpoint of assumption, man finds ease more natural than dis-ease. He ceases to get rid of disease as a reality and contemplates the Son of God living in the perfect ease of Spirit. One moment of this realization and his disease has vanished into nothingness, for the perfect Self is thereby revealed and made manifest.

From the standpoint of assumption, man gains the actual, concrete results he has failed to accomplish by the process of imagination he formerly used. Are you afraid to follow in the steps of the Master and assume your divine rights and see them into manifestation? Are you afraid to accept the results of consciously accepting your birthright?

The "worm of the dust" finally discovers that he can do nothing to change or better himself, for he is a product of the dual belief in good and evil. Working with the body and personality is exactly the same thing.

No matter what you have been, done, or left undone, when the Christ has been recognized as your true Self, all former limitations fade away. Thousands of sincere souls, seeking the light, have spent years trying to better the condition of the "worm in the dust," trying to make "John Smith" a better man—healthier, richer, or happier—but have accomplished little. The caterpillar cannot change except from within. No good trying to make a caterpillar fly; it is impossible. A complete change has to take place, a transformation. Jesus the carpenter becomes the Christ, the Son of the living God, with all power. The caterpillar becomes the butterfly.

Certain laws have to be heeded. If the caterpillar fails to close itself within its cocoon, it might have the desire and the capacity to become a butterfly but would be utterly unable to do so because it failed to heed the law of secrecy. To lose the personality, secrecy is necessary. The change would be too great for the prying, doubting Thomas to participate in the glory of it. "See that ye tell no man" wraps a cloak about the one who suddenly begins the process of *assumption*, just as the cocoon is built around the grub that is to become the butterfly. Later, that which acts as a cloak of protection becomes a hindrance and is cast off. The scaffolding is torn down finally, in order that the perfect structure can be seen. The secrecy gives up its perfect manifestation; then man may say, "Go and show John."

The change that is made between the grub and the butterfly is tremendous, but it is nothing as compared to the change that takes place in the one who evolves from the John Smith personality (the worm of the dust) into the Son of the living God. What was impossible to John Smith is divinely natural to the New Idea. As the butterfly seeks a new mode and means of expression after it has given up its caterpillar state of existence, so the man who has *assumed* his Sonship, and seen it out to manifestation, moves into a new heaven and a new earth. The butterfly takes no cognizance of its former expression—no worrying over its mistakes, shortcomings, omissions, and fears. They are nothing. The new expression is so far removed from the old, it is as a dream. The former things shall pass away—"they shall be remembered no more, neither shall they come into mind." So the new Son of the living God, moving into his *new* kingdom of expression, drops off all worries and fears, the cause and effect of the John Smith personality.

"Be still, and know that I am God" takes on a new meaning: be still and *assume* the glories of this new estate. Assume them in the secret place—easily, naturally. Assume them and rest them in the silence. "Be wise as serpents, harmless as doves." Know nothing, see nothing, hear nothing; then you will know all, see all, and hear all.

Come away from the noisy personality who wants to change the John Smith and heal him and make him prosper. You are the Son of the living God, and when you recognize this, you are through with the foolish idea of making demonstrations. You will see the constant outpouring of the substance of God through the new idea by the *assumption* of the Son. One in all and All in One. Be still and serenely assume the God-given qualities and hide them deep in the cocoon of silence. Then will they burst forth as glorious, freed expressions.

"Be not afraid; it is I." The very *I* that is able to *assume* Its God inheritance is at this time speaking to you: "Behold, I stand at the door and knock." It is already there, awaiting recognition. It does not need healing, prosperity, being made happy or joyous. It is already these things. Identify yourself with It. "Acquaint now thyself with him and be at peace." "Know ye not that ye are gods?" Do you know it? If so, when will you *assume* the God-like qualities and see them into manifestation? Be still—build the secret cocoon about you; presently you shall be transformed by the renewing of your mind.

Chapter III

I Am Here, I Am There,
I Am Everywhere

"I am here, I am there, I am everywhere." I am within all, within every fiber, nerve, and cell of your being. I am in the inanimate as well as the animate—I am everywhere.

I am everything and everywhere. Call upon Me and see if I will not open the windows of divine substance. I AM THAT I AM—that particular I AM Consciousness which should come to this condition or situation to make its nothingness appear, to cause it to release the power that lies hidden there and which has caused you to fear.

I am All in All—I am everywhere. No matter wither you go, into what locality, I am there—I have gone before you because I am already there and always have been there. I have already caused myself to be so impressed upon you that you find everything already prepared before you arrive. You find everything answered before you ask. You find everything supplied before the need. It is well with you—do you hear?—irrespective of person, place, or thing. It is well with you, irrespective of teachings of any nature whatsoever. I AM … I AM … I AM.

I am the lost word which is hidden within your consciousness, which *is* your consciousness, veiled over by a mystification of human senses. In judging from appearances, you have lost true values and have accepted shadows as realities. I am the lost word, the Word before which the doors of the universe fly open—doors in the impassible walls of human obstacles; doors that lead out on highways never charted by the human sense because of its limitations. Doors that belong to the palaces of the kings fly open at My coming, and the riches of that which is Caesar's are laid before Me, to take and do with as *I* like.

I am here, *I* am there, *I* am everywhere. It is well.

The new voyage on which you are about to embark is already prepared; all the minutest details have been taken care of. Arise, take no thought; all these things shall be added to the unafraid one. Do you hear? You who read this page? You? The endless planning and trying to arrange things suddenly ceases. The government shall be upon his shoulders, the government of your life, and all is well. Only the personal attitude can keep you out of this beautiful, restful experience. Be not afraid: "It is I." Why should you be afraid to accept your good here and now, instead of waiting for the harvest? Have *I* not told you over and over again, "Look again"—the fields are white, the laborers are few. Thrust in the sickle. Reap, you who read this page. You!

Reap the fullness of Life everywhere present. Not one thing shall be hidden from you. When you come to recognize the Allness of Life, there will be no place for sin, disease, and death, and you shall find a new thing working in your members which will be above both health and sickness, a new consciousness which is not the result of evil overcome, but which is the out-picturing of the Spirit, which is of too pure eyes to behold iniquity.

The healed man is perhaps better than the sick man, but he is still swinging between something and nothing. If he wishes to stop the swinging between the pair of opposites, he will have to move up to the place of recognition of the All-Presence and there abide in a state of changeless bliss. His ability, then, will not be to demonstrate the word but to bring the living presence of the word into visibility. This is your power; it is the power which was given to the child, in consciousness—the ability to accept the Good that has been prepared for him. Do you hear? I speak the word of healing for you at this moment.

There is but the *Now*—it is Now that I write. It is Now that you read, and at this divine instant of the All-Now, I speak from out of these pages and say:

> Rise up and walk; open your eyes and see the glorious finished mystery; open your ears and hear the things which human lips cannot utter; stretch forth your arm of strength and accomplish that which you will. Go your way into expression. It is well with you. Be whole; be free; be newly born.

You who are reading this page, do you hear? Do you hear? Do you hear? In the glorious All-Now, it is well with you. Rise and declare from the housetops your being. It is wonderful! It is wonderful! It is wonderful! Even the wrath of man shall praise thee; even the thing which has seemed so untoward shall rise and sing thy glory. The limited personal Jesus shall praise the Christ within your consciousness. You shall call it from the housetops of your being by telling it in secret to your soul—by pure recognition of the All-Presence in the All-Now.

Human language fails to express anything like the Joy of the All-Now, but between the lines you will find the Spirit that will accomplish this for you. Be still; the unuttered word is the Word of God which shall not, cannot, and has not the ability to return unto you void. For the Word of God is fulfillment pressing toward your consciousness for expression. The word which speaks it into existence is the actual recognition of the Presence everywhere.

I am here, *I* am there, *I* am everywhere. To recognize this is to understand without further difficulty how it is that you can now reach out across the universe and touch Me in another being and cause that being to take on the splendid sense of health, happiness, and prosperity that you formerly tried to make happen by beseeching special favors of Me. The Sons of God shout for joy—you cannot help it. *"Blessings, blessings, blessings, so many you cannot count them."* Blessings so many. Like the deluge of golden mist that fills the valley after a storm, you are filled with this invisible-visible substance, and the light from this consciousness causes all the evil shadows of human belief to recede. It is well with you. Blessings, blessings, blessings, so many you cannot count them. Do you hear? Do you hear? Not the cold human words, but the Spirit of that which sets aside every human law, however conceived or made. Blessings that come from the grace of God, pouring into expression into your life in the All-Now, in the All-Presence.

Be still outwardly and shout for joy within until it has shattered the walls of your prison. Do you see? If you once glimpse the All-Presence in the All-Now, you will begin to see that *I* am not only here and there and everywhere, but *I* am everything and partake of the nature of everything through this great Oneness. *I* am everything and everybody—*I* am All.

I speak to you, and for this reason comes this message into your hand. From this instant, *I* am into manifestation in your life as a real, living factor—not as a far-off God but as the very life of your life, the great connecting link between you and everything manifest on the earth. It is well; be not afraid. It is *I*.

I have many hidden things to show you when you can be still. One by one, the clamoring voices of argument, revenge, and resentment will have screamed themselves lifeless. That which can rend you must come out of you, even though you fall as one dead, and dead you will be to human babbling. This which can rend you sore must come out of you so that you can soar to new heights which were impossible with the former baggage. Let go, give up, and call down into manifestation the blessing of the All-Now and the All-Presence. *I* am here (right while you are

21

reading, right while I am writing), *I* am there, *I* am everywhere. The coming and going of things is only in the
human thought. Nothing passes away in the reality of the
Real. There is nothing to be destroyed or hurt or made right.

When you have ascended into heaven and glimpsed
the eternal, perfect harmony of that consciousness without
beginning or ending, you will descend into the hell of
your human thinking and bring with you the All-Presence
and see this hell self-consumed. You will see the fire of
evil wiped out by the blaze of life. You will merely bring
the recognition of that which is in heaven unto earth, or
out into the manifest world, and see it change. You will
see a whole city appear, with the evaporation of a fog of
human thinking and belief, and your heaven unfold before
you out of the mystification of your human thought.

Right where you are is holy ground, for *I* am here, *I*
am there, *I* am everywhere.

Unlatch the latchets of your sandals; let go of the
human reasoning or the how, why, when, and where; let
go of all systems of Truth and drink deep of the living
water of inspiration which is wordless and unutterable. *I*
shall impress you with that which is. "Stand and deliver"
… "He who hears obeys."

"When the Son of Man cometh, shall he find faith on
the earth?" You have to answer that for yourself. Perhaps
you have already answered it in the negative for the rest
of the world. But it has nothing to do with the rest of the
world; it has only to do with your world. When the revelation cometh to you, when *I* come to you and speak,
even as *I* am speaking at this instant, shall that *I* find
faith—recognition on the earth—in the manifest realm of
your earth?

While you are looking for evil in the world to overcome, you are making so much noise you cannot hear Me
as *I* stand at your door and knock. It is well; be not afraid.
One day the awakening comes, and then you take your

pearl of great price and run away and bury it in a field, in a new state of consciousness—and you tell no man about it. And you know why. The deepening of consciousness takes place and with it the glorious accompanying manifestation. Have *I* not said to you in many ways, "If a man lose his life he shall find it"? If you lose the personality, letting it be swallowed up in the I AM, then will you lose also all the human law pertaining to that personality. The problems of that personality will then be of no concern to you, for they will cease to exist. The personality is on the plane of cause and effect—the "four months to the harvest," the "as ye sow, so shall ye reap." But when you are lost in Me, you find your real life, the life everlasting. Literally some will find this and appropriate it and be translated into the new and wondrous Spirit.

Remember, *I* have said unto you, "The last enemy that shall be overcome is death." When you lose your limited personal sense of life in the All-Life, you lose the sense of disease and evil, and without disease, death cannot come into manifestation. Hence, the last enemy, the last belief in a power outside of the All-Presence, is swallowed up. Death is swallowed up in victory, in Life, and you shall say, "Whereas before, I was dead, *now* (the only) *I* am alive."

Take away the condemnation from your world; bathe it in the new Light of Love and Life. When you cease to look for evil, evil will cease to manifest to you.

> Kick the hell of rigid things from 'neath your feet and leap through space; and space shall hold you with the thrilling flux of life ascending; and hold you more complete in every part than did the rigid coils ye flung behind you.

The rigid coils of human thinking—the age-old beliefs and laws that have seemed like the coils of a python, crushing the very life out of you! These shall finally be put from you by being divested of their power. There is that upward rising, that quickening, that going to the Father, which is the recognition that lifts up to the Mount. "Underneath are the everlasting arms." The everlasting power is with you and in you and through you—the great changelessness of the Law of God, which is:

As above, so below;
As within, so without.

No place can you go where *I* am not. If you take the wings of the morning and fly to the uttermost parts of the earth, there am *I*; or into hell, there am *I*. *I* only have to be recognized to set aflame the bush by the wayside. *I* have myriad ways of speaking to you—when the scales of a double universe have dropped from your eyes. I AM THAT I AM. Do you hear? Nothing is hard to Me.

You who have struggled all night with the Angel shall at last have the bandage of human belief torn from your eyes, and you shall loose it and let it go. So many have tried this by first recognizing that the Angel had power which was working against them, and then, in trying to let go, found it practically impossible to do so. Do you not see that the only reason a problem has power is because you feed it constantly with your thought? The more your attention is upon it the greater it becomes to you; then one day, you recognize the startling fact that you are sustaining it like a parasite which is mocking the meat it is feeding upon, and you take from it the nourishment of thought and find that in so doing you have loosened the only hold it had upon you. Do you see? You who read this page? You?

In the spaceless and timeless center of your soul, you will see the nothingness of the dust of human existence; you will see that the thousand years have been but a day and that you stand gloriously revealed to yourself, and it is this inner revelation which causes the human manifestation to come to higher and more perfect proportions and expression. The effect will take care of itself. The out-picturing of the state recognized within will automatically be made manifest. When the mind lets go of what it has been holding in the hand, the hand lets go and drops the article automatically, even though it was holding on with all might and main before.

Do you see that the results that follow are the signs which follow and which do not precede? When you are not looking for signs, for results, it will be because you are completely satisfied that the law of God never fails, and therefore, any anxiety or thought you take regarding the outcome of the inner vision is totally wasted and in many cases acts as a mist which obscures the truth which should appear.

I have passed you often on the highways of life, and you have failed to see or hear Me because you are eternally looking to the outward shell. Remember that *I* speak through any avenue that is free enough to let Me into expression. *I* do not always come with purple and fine linen or the approval of a church; *I* come in the manner in which you can best see Me. But if you are hypnotized to the outside, to the appearances, then you will pass Me by.

Fear not! When you are ready, *I* will do the works through you. When you are ready to let go of the limiting sense of things about you and the limiting personality with which you have identified yourself, you will see Me.

I am here, *I* am there, *I* am everywhere—blessings, blessings, blessings, so many you cannot count them.

Do you hear? You who read this page? You?

Chapter IV

The Laughter of God

God has made me to laugh,
so that all that hear will laugh with me.

Deep in my soul, I hear the Laughter of God, ringing in silvery cadences through the timbers of my being, breaking the human bonds and limitations as a strong yet gentle wind in the forest sweeps aside the strands of cobweb. The hard, fast knots that I had tied slipped loose, and the snarls of beliefs broke free. The river of my human life, frozen by a thousand and one false ideas and teachings, broke joyously into expression and went bounding to the infinite sea of Life, to be lost and found at the same time.

One dark cave of fear after another was illuminated by the light of this laughter, and swampy areas of sick thoughts were dried up instantly. Parched sands of hopelessness and futile efforts were drenched by the living waters, sucked in—absorbed instantly like a wave breaking on the sands. God laughing at me and my puny efforts to make things happen—to make heaven appear; to attain the Sonship. Not the laugh of derision but of infinite compassion, a laughter so deep and sweet, so pure and glorious that everything in the nature of struggle gave way before it.

The breath of that glorious laughter blew all the dirty rags of personal teaching and self-aggrandizement away from me, and at first the fierce joy that proceeded from the unheard-heard peals of laughter made me afraid—afraid that everything worthwhile was being taken from me and that I should be naked. But no sooner had the filthy rags of personality blown free than I was clothed in a panoply of light, and in this glorious raiment of light I saw for the first time the glory of the Spirit made flesh.

I stood before the infinite peals of laughter, which flowed through all creation like floods of golden mist, filled with speechless wonder at the beauty of the world I had lived in—which had been invisible because of my separation, because of my personal ideas about attainment. I was as a child with a small measure at the seaside, trying to carry off a little water when the whole sea was at my disposal, and I understood for the first time the exhaustless sea of substance about me and that the idea of hoarding was but a childish fear grown into a Goliath by false teaching and beliefs. I suddenly became aware that the substance was everywhere, in everything, out of everything, and the only place of lack was in the hypnotic state of belief—and I alone created and moved in this vacuum.

And the glorious laughter rolled on, searching the very joints and marrow of me—dislodging every belief in fear, sickness, or age. As it swept over me and through me and round about me, I was amazed with the wonder of it—the fierce, terrible thing which was at the same time so beautiful and free. The wonder of it kept singing through my soul, as veil after veil of belief was rent asunder and new kingdoms stood revealed. And the whole thing was as if one just saw a little deeper, as one looks through the surface reflection on a river and sees the pebbles and shells below, that was all. Only the Laughter made this possible, for it cleared away all the effort and straining which, in its attempt to see God, had been halted at the reflection on the surface instead of gazing into the limpid, glorious depth of Infinity.

The Voice, as its honeyed tones flowed out like a burst of sunshine through storm clouds, was so unlabored, so untrammeled, and so divinely indifferent that it seemed to envelop me with an instant realization that all was well. No matter how many struggles had been made, no matter how many mistakes, how many shortcomings, how many failures, how long the belief or how short the hate, it was all swept aside as nothing. The glorious, divine ease with which it was expressed made dis-ease impossible. It was the overturning and overturning that had to take place before He, the Laughing One, could come into expression. The people of God are a people of joy, and it is not until they hear this God-Laughter in their souls that they have attained to their heritage.

What of this race that speaks of the Kingdom and doing the Father's work and uses all the language of the Truth, and at the same time sows seeds of fear and hellish inventions? What is this race that is always seeking evil to destroy, like a weasel seeks out a rat? What is the hopelessness they preach—that on one hand you are the Sons of God and on the other you must fight against evil of every sort and nature? "Ah, yes—but, if, and maybe ..." They roll these stumbling blocks under their tongues with a wise twinkle in their eyes, as much as to say, "Yes, it is all true, but it comes only with hard labor and long study, and it is not for such as you, sinner and worm of the dust that you are, until you have purified yourself in the fount of my wisdom and paid me personal homage."

And it is then that the Magdalene hears the Laughter of God and is clean and free—and in an instant, too. It is when the cripple hears the Laughter of God that he leaps to his feet and runs away praising the living God. And it is when you—no matter where you are or what you are, no matter what you have done or left undone—hear the Laughter of the God within and the God without that you will crash through the gates of hell and find heaven, no matter what these gates may be—person, place, or thing.

One moment's recognition that you are the Son of the living God, and you have attuned your ear for the Laughter of God which will put to flight all the stupid ideas of mine and thine and free you into an expression that you have not yet dreamed of. How can you restrain the joy that fills you when you hear this laughter which, when it is heard, causes the winter of your discontent to break into full fruition; which causes you to see literally that "before they call I will answer" is not a bit of euphonious language but a positive, living, glowing fact.

"I was afraid," and therefore you were driven out of the Garden of Life. You have been afraid that God will punish you, that it is too good to be true, that you are not ready, that it comes by great learning—and so you are still without the portals of your own kingdom, trying every way but the only way to re-enter. Many there be who try the way of violence and many who expect to ride in on the skirts of another. There are some so foolish as to invite this.

Why do you not stop trying to get things, trying to learn how to get power, place? Why do you not come away from the man whose breath is in his nostrils—you who read this page—and go within and hear the Laughter of God and know that "it does not matter," that the things which gave you great concern are all swept away into the dump heap? The sooner you learn this the sooner you will see they have no value. And one time, when you take away their value, they are possible of attainment to you. You profess to be a follower of the Master. If you in any way believe this, you will begin to listen for the Laughter of God through your whole being and will know that the Laughter of God sets you free from the snarling discontent of the tower of Babel in which you have been living.

Presently, as you listen for this Laughter, you will hear it, and gradually you will begin laughing—billows of laughter, silently-audible laughter that will shatter one limitation after another; laughter filled with the divine indifference which knows that the Universe is filled with God, and only God, and that to recognize this will cause this laughter to flow into expression and shatter the belief in sin, sickness, and death. When this belief is shattered in

29

you, the pictures of this on your universe are dissipated and are no more, and even the place thereof is no more. You will know why there can be naught but laughter in the kingdom of heaven. What good of words or arguments? What, in human sense, is a lecture worth on the subject of Laughter as compared to one glorious, sudden peal of joy released by a God-soul and picked up by all those in hearing distance?

Gradually, as you learn of the Laughter of God and join in with the glory of the Sons of the living God, then you will laugh at yourself. You will perhaps go back and laugh all the mistakes and faults and limitations out of existence. You will stand with your glorious feet on the mountaintops of Self-revelation, laughing at your universe and with your universe and laughing in words: "It is wonderful, it is wonderful, it is wonderful."

"Let the filthy be filthy still." Some may read into the Laughter of God a belief in carelessness and indifference, and some consecrated souls may rail and tear their hair and say that it is encouraging license and making nothing of sin, in order that one may indulge in sin, and so on. For them, this message is not.

He that hath ears shall hear what the Scripture saith unto the churches, and only he that hath a single eye is through with trying to twist meanings to suit personal ends. But he that hath the consciousness of the Son of the living God shall not find it strange that he that "is of too pure eyes to behold iniquity" should laugh at the belief in it that has bound men for so long. This divine disregard does not in any way encourage license, but gives liberty to the Sons of God. It breaks up the dank morasses of human belief and reveals itself as heaven, a state of consciousness which finds not happiness at the disposal of sin, health at the disposal of sickness, and harmony at the disposal of inharmony, but finds these pairs of opposites swept away. It finds man the individual Son of the living

God, experiencing power and wisdom such as could not be put in human language.

The impress of the Divine upon the human causes the human to express in what, to the unenlightened thought, may seem to be a supernatural way. The how and why and when are all vested in the limited human concept of life. You who read this page—when are you going to start laughing the Laughter of God? When are you going to join in the glorious chorus which is already encircling the globe and which has for its password "It is wonderful"? You cannot stop this laughter once it is started; you will shatter the belief in disease in thousands as you go along your way—not by a poor, half-hearted way of beseeching God, but with the ringing Laughter of God in your Soul, which knows no sickness, sin, or disease, and hence cannot look upon it. And in this very knowledge, it will impress the consciousness with the eternal well-being of the Son of the living God.

The man, if he hear the Laughter—that is, if he be willing to hear it instead of accepting the pinched human concepts of his human reasonings—shall break the bounds of his limitations, crash through the gates of brass, shake off the shackles of belief, burst through the prison bars of his own making, and find himself free, free, free, and find his soul ringing with laughter and with the song "It is wonderful."

Whoever you are who reads this page—you who sit in prison houses of disease, sin, and unhappiness—listen, listen, listen. *I* am the door of attainment. He will "fill thy mouth with laughing, and thy lips with rejoicing." *I* am the door to this glorious Laughter of God— *I* am the way to the eternal bliss and harmony of the Sons of the living God. No matter where this finds you, nothing is hopeless or helpless. This joyous Laughter of the recognition of God, here and now, of the Finished Kingdom—of the sudden discovery that Jesus was not a liar but a truthsayer, a concrete truthsayer, when he said, "The kingdom of heaven is at hand—it is within you"—will cause this kingdom to descend out of the clouds of your belief and be real.

How can you help laughing silently and audibly the Laughter of God and see its ringing notes shatter the silly arguments about life? The wisdom of man is foolish in the eyes of God. Why try to measure the inspiration of the Almighty against any manmade teaching! "I will make you fishers of men." *I*, the I AM, when once discovered, will make the one who discovers It a fisher of men. Who can resist the Laughter of God—the fearless Laughter of God, ringing through the universe, sweeping all the debris of human belief out of the way? No matter if it be thousands of years old and hoary with the respect of mankind. Not one stone shall remain in place. The very foundations of the human belief shall be shaken in order that the true cornerstone, which has been rejected up to now, shall be laid.

Yes, the stone—the very stone that the Master gave to us, the philosopher's stone, if you will, which we have rejected because to accept it would have been to overthrow great temples of human reasoning—will finally be made the head stone of the temple of Truth. You are the temple of the living God, and from out the inner recesses of your being proceeds the Laughter of God. "The Sons of God shout for joy." You will shout for joy, not because of victory over evil, but because you have at last realized that the kingdom of heaven is not a place of overcoming evil but of revelation which is above the belief of a divided universe. "Awake, thou that sleepest, and Christ shall give thee light."

And I heard the Laughter of God in the Soul of my very being—ringing in glorious cadence throughout my universe, causing me suddenly to burst into a glorious laughter which was full of praise, full of wonder, full of wonder and amazement at that which I had missed through looking through a glass, darkly. "Arise, shine, for thy light has come." Do you hear? It is wonderful! It is wonderful! It is wonderful! Heaven and earth are full of Thee—sin, sickness, and death have vanished away. I *hear* the Laughter of God ringing in the deep recesses of your soul, you who read this page. I see the moving finger writing across all the worries and fears of a lifetime "It does not matter," and I see this laughter writing the things of beauty over the walls of your temple and casting a glorious, glistening white robe—a seamless robe of attainment—over you.

And at last I hear you laughing from the mountain peak as you go on your way, without thought of scrip or purse or robe or ring or upper chamber, and long before you have reached your destination, the Laughter of God in your soul has gone ahead and made ready the upper chamber, and the Host has come out to receive you. Do you hear? You who read this page? You?

Chapter V

Your Divine Heritage

"Claim your right and press your claim."

What is your right? Who are you? Until you fully recognize these two points, you are merely playing about with an affirmation, merely toying with some words. Thousands have spent years of their lives claiming "All that the Father hath is mine" and had difficulty finding enough to pay for a week's lodging and food.

Beloved, how long will you wait without, seeking for that which is in plain sight? How long will you try to make God do that which is already done? When will you identify yourself with the Christ within, the Son of the most High, and begin to see the right—the Divine Heritage, the joy that will come to you when you realize that life is not just one long, tiresome job of demonstrating God? Thousands are today rising each morning and getting busy knowing the truth about God and His universe, hoping thereby to overcome some of the fiendish conditions of the flesh—and finding themselves defeated.

Who are you? Were you created by God, or by some erring human concept which has thrown you into a hell of change, and then given you a glimmer of light which says that if by your prayers you can establish the fact that there is a God, perhaps He will give you a crust of bread? You have been taught as much—conceived in sin, brought forth in iniquity, worm of the dust, miserable sinner. Where does the Divine Heritage come in? Where does the Child of God find its own? Nowhere and everywhere. Nowhere so long as you are looking for him in some far-off place, and everywhere when you recognize the presence here and now.

Now are we the Sons of God—right now. When a man hears the word *now* in its true sense, he finds he has been spelling it backward and that in reality the *now* understood means *won*. You have won the Sonship and all that goes with it when you understand the *now* of Spirit. You are not a mixture of matter and spirit. Ice and steam are the same in essence, but as steam, the water is lighter than ice. You are not a material thing separated from God, but a being of pure Spirit. If God had been clay in the first instance, everything that He evolved would have been made of clay. But we find Him as pure Spirit, all-inclusive, and hence, the creation must of necessity be Spirit.

You, as the highest manifestation of this power, are made of the all-inclusive substance of mind called Spirit. You are the Son, or the center of manifestation, where all the innate qualities of God pour out into expression. It is asking no special dispensation or favor of God for you, as the Son, to claim your right and press your claim. It is merely recognizing that which innately belongs to you.

The name of the Prince of Wales is Edward David Windsor, but the power is vested in his claiming his rights as the Prince of Wales and pressing his claim into expression. You are a prince by the name of I Am—only you fail to recognize this and hence beg at the open fount, wondering if, by beseeching the tyrant you worship through fear, He will give you enough to live on. The less you ask for the harder it is to get—not because of any stinginess of the Power but by reason of its tremendous affluence. If you hold a pint cup in Niagara Falls, you will come away with it empty—not because of the lack of water but because of too much water. The force of the water dashes everything out as fast as it gets in because the measure is too small. Your poor little vision of what belongs to you keeps you from having the abundance of Spirit. You can have all and all be left.

"All that the Father hath is mine." Where is the Father? What is the Father? If you look at this in terms of Jesus' words, you find that the Father is within you and you have everything, or all, that your Father has. Putting this through the limited beliefs of personality causes you to partake of the good, bad, or indifferent states of your consciousness. All that you have in your consciousness—all that you conceive the Father within you to be—is all that you actually have into manifestation.

If your room is ten feet square, you can have the entire radio concert just the same as a man with a room a thousand feet square, and this can go on indefinitely and still all of it remain. The measure that you hold to the universe is all that can possibly come into manifestation. If you are dissatisfied with the results of your daily life, it cannot be rectified from without, but a better concept of the Father within—taking attention entirely away from the appearances—will enable you to bring out what you formerly called demonstrations. You will begin to see that enlarging the borders of your tent means becoming more conscious of the Power within and discovering its unlimited capacities—which are up and beyond anything that you can think of.

All things are possible to Me, but nothing is possible to me. I doubt if a great portion of the people in the world would be affected one way or the other by the name *David Windsor*, but most anyone is interested in the name *the Prince of Wales*—and yet they are one and the same person. If he did not recognize this fact, another would certainly usurp his rights. Even though he be born to the place, if he did not recognize this, he would never have the power of it. Even though you are born the Son of God, with unlimited power and happiness within your rights, until you recognize this you function along as John Smith or some other person, ignorant of the glorious freedom of the Sons of God, and you will beg for a crust when you might be sitting at the overflowing table of the infinite Spirit.

Joy comes when you make a clear line of demarcation between the John Smith and the Christ. You begin at once to appropriate the rights of the Son of God. In pressing your claim, you do not drive a hard bargain—you do not fight. In this sense, *pressing* means merely standing firm on the points that you know to be true and turning not to the right or left. It means saluting no man as you pass along the way (saluting no belief of doubt or appearance as you go forward into expression of the Son of God).

"Claim your right and press your claim," says Father Divine, and shows by his magnificent example that the Son of God hath power on earth to forgive sins (to correct the ignorance of human belief). And then follow the magnificent works without number, until millions of blessings are pouring down about everybody. When I attempt to count my blessings, they are as numerous as the sands of the sea. Your blessings, Son of the living God, are so numerous that you have no time to contemplate the lack of anything, and when you attempt to count the blessings, you find the lack has been swallowed up in abundance, and you are free, here and now, as the Son of the living God.

It is wonderful! It is wonderful! It is wonderful! "O taste and see that the Lord is good." "Prove me ... and see if I will not open windows in heaven, and pour out a blessing you will not be able to receive."

Where is heaven? It is a state of consciousness. What is the *me*? It is the I AM within you; hence, the windows that are to be opened are in your own consciousness, and the blessings that are to be poured out are the ideas which will pour out through your own mind into the manifest world of expression. *"It is wonderful. Millions and millions of blessings are yours."* Do you hear, Son of God?

Stop this useless trying to seek Me after the loaves and fishes; find Me as the pure substance of Spirit, and you will hear the joyous command, "Heretofore ye have asked for nothing; now ask, that your joy might be full." Not nearly full, but full to overflowing! Do you begin to see what Father Divine means when he says, "Press your claim" after having claimed your rights? You are one with the mighty sea of substance.

As the wave is one with the ocean—never for one instant separated—and rises and loses itself in the ocean, so man finds that:

> Losing his life he finds it,
> And by saving his life he loses it.

When you lose your little personal sense of life, you will find the one Life—that which is wonderful, the life that is *won now*—the heaven here and now.

What have you to worry over, beloved? A new day, a new start, a new idea. No matter where this finds you, no matter into what depths you have fallen or to what dizzy heights you have climbed, you have the wonderful chance of finding the glorious true Self within and claiming your rights and pressing your claim as the Son of the living God.

Just imagine what this means. It means that there is no more personal effort to do and to be. It means that the Father within is responsible, and it means that the I AM goes before your John Smith and makes the way clear and perfect. Do you see why you suddenly awaken to the realities of being and begin to take your good out of the universe?

For as Father Divine says, "I am here, and I am there, and I am everywhere," so you find that the power in the wave is not separated from the ocean but moves through the wave, an impersonal power. The power in you is not a personal possession of health, happiness, or prosperity but is an impersonal power which is merely pouring itself out into expression through the visible means supplied. Do you see, then, how all men (Sons of God) are equal? We have been hypnotized to the belief that we were body, with a little health or power shut up within; with a little capacity to earn money; with a little wit to psychologize people out of money or things. And now we are awake to the fact that the power is pouring through us, never the same and always the same.

As we go toward the fountain at the distance, we have not seen the same picture two minutes in succession; the water has been changing constantly yet has held the same form. So it is with the Spirit. It is a constant change of changeless power coming into manifestation. You are the Son of God, and the great Power is here and there and everywhere. If you go into the desert, you have but to recognize this to find it blossoming as a rose. *I* am here and *I* am there and *I* am everywhere. It is wonderful—it is truly wonderful. Blessings, blessings, blessings.

Do you see, beloved, the gift—the complete wholeness? For this *is* (right here and now) Life eternal, that they might know Me. To know the Me, the I AM, and to identify yourself with this is to experience the Life eternal which needs nothing. Can you conceive of Spirit being burned, drowned, killed, aided, or assisted in any way by matter? To know yourself as the Son is to experience the freedom of the Son of God—to experience the power of decreeing a thing and seeing it come to pass. The recognition—re-cognition, cognizing again that which has always been true, the divine remembrance of your rightful heritage—is what will restore to you the lost substance of life, is what will bring to you the robe, the ring, and the fatted calf.

To him that hath shall be given, and to him that hath not shall be taken away. You have into manifestation exactly what you have in consciousness—good, bad, or indifferent. Why waste any further time trying to change the outside condition, when it is held in manifestation by the inner state of consciousness?

To him that hath shall be given—because he will take, be this good, bad, or indifferent manifestation. A man with a consciousness full of troubles always gets more troubles, and he finds them everywhere. It is what he finds to be true, and so he must find it into manifestation.

No wonder the prophet asked, "What have you in your house?" What have you in your house, your consciousness? You have just what you conceive the Father within to be, and you cannot increase this until you begin to recognize the nature of the pure substance of Spirit from which all things come into manifestation. Until you recognize the true Self and stop trying to doctor up an old body or condition, you cannot know the glory of the Son of God. You are not an old creature patched up. You are a new creature in Christ Jesus. You are a new, perfect manifestation. To recognize this is to claim your rights and press your claim by the serene power of the Almighty.

Every perfect gift "cometh down from the Father of lights, with whom there is no change, neither shadow of turning." Where is the Father? How long will you look for Him in some far-off locality? How long will you seek among the husks for the substance of life? Every gift that is to come to you as John Smith will proceed out of the center of the I AM consciousness within yourself.

Behold, *I* am "he that should come." I AM THAT I AM has sent me into expression. It is wonderful, it is wonderful. Blessings, blessings, blessings. *I* am the Son of the living God.

Claim your rights and press your claim. Son of the living God, I salute you! Arise! Leave the filth of your human reasoning and go unto your Father within. Let the filthy be filthy still. Let all those who wish to sell the Word of God continue to do so. Let those who want to argue continue their arguments. Let those judges and spiritual busybodies cast their stones.

Go thy way; it is well with thee. The new secret has been revealed to you; do you hear? Peace be unto you. It is well. Now and always. Claim your right and press your claim. It is well with you. Now and always. Son of the living God, arise and go thy way into Expression. Now is the time. Now is the Day of Salvation. Now are we the Sons of God. Now are millions of blessings yours.

Be still ... be still ... be still. It is wonderful, it is wonderful, it is wonderful. Blessings, blessings, blessings.

Chapter VI

My Name Is Wonderful

*My name is wonderful, the mighty, the
counselor, the Prince of Peace. Of my reign
there shall be no end—the government
shall be upon my shoulders.*

Call upon My name and *I* shall answer thee. That is
why, when you call the word *wonderful*, the very soul of
the idea rises and shakes off its grave clothes. To call it
wonderful, though it be coated over with appearances of
death and disease, of sin or poverty, is to see the sleeping
Lazarus arise—not from death but from beliefs—and shed
his limiting bandages and bonds.

Call upon My name and *I* shall answer. My name is
wonderful—the mighty, the name of the I Aм, the eternally
present tense of life, the *eternal first Person*, from which
emanates the unspoken-spoken word and the invisible-
visible. Call upon Me and *I* will answer you; yea, even
before you call, *I* will answer. *I* am before all the beliefs
of limiting human beliefs. Though a man were dead, yet
shall he live again; though you were dead in the hypnotism
of a thousand years of belief, yet shall you live again in
this truth and wonder after wonder pass over you.

Self-revelation—revelation of hidden talents of which
you, the John Smith, have never dreamed; revelation of
capacities and opportunities which were beyond your fond-
est dreams come to the surface and are yours for the mere
acceptance. It is wonderful.

"Salute no man that thou passest upon the highway,"
lest he try to foist upon you a personal teaching—lest he
try to turn you aside by his own holier-than-thou brand of
teaching. Look within, and look away from the fleeting

man whose breath is in his nostrils. "Look unto me (the Christ within) and be ye saved, all the ends of the earth" from the dire effects of your beliefs. Though you be red like crimson with beliefs in sin, sickness, and limitation, yet shall you be white as snow—because you were always that way and always shall be that way. Pretty soon you shall see Me and shall glory in the revelation and see the glorious possibilities of the Sons of God. Then will you drink deep of the Water of Life, and go forth and smite the rock of human intelligence and make it gush forth the waters in such floods and abundance that it will cause the parched desert of your life to blossom as a rose. Do you hear? Do you heed? You are the Child of the living God. Your name is Wonderful. Call upon Me, and *I* shall answer—yes, before you call, *I* will answer.

All the human reasoning goes down like a house of cards before the Self-revelation. What of this wisdom which today is true and tomorrow is found to be nothing and is cast into the furnace of oblivion? All sin is but ignorance of Me. It is the conscious or unconscious ignoring of My Presence. As soon as you understand, the results of your ignorance, or ignoring Me, disappear and you find harmony. As soon as you have the answer to a problem, you have no problem. You cannot have answer and problem at the same time; a problem is only a problem as long as it remains unanswered. And the problems of life remain unanswered until you realize that *I* am the answer to everything, for all problems are merely the ignorance, the ignoring, of Me—your inner Lord, your true Self, and the real You.

My wisdom is foolishness in the eyes of man, whose breath is in his nostrils. He has only that breath for a few years, and then it gives out and he falls by the way. Verily, verily I say unto you, "You must be born again"— awakened to the Truth of Being, which will cause you to see through the limited beliefs and make you shout to the most foreboding evil that the belief-world is capable of presenting to you: "It is wonderful." It is the name of the I AM, the Father-Mother, Divine Neuter, or All-Complete. It is wonderful and, when recognized, comes out into manifestation, and One with this consciousness is a majority. Do you hear? "Put up your sword." You do not need to fight. "Set yourselves ... and see."

Be still, beloved. *I* am at this instant revealing My (Your) self to you—wordless impressions, nameless glories—revelation after revelation. *I* am bringing to your sight the luster of the pearl of great price. Once you have seen this, you will know that nothing matters and that everything matters. You will know the serenity of your soul and see the fleeting shadows of the human belief disappear, because you have but to call upon Me then and have the immediate answer.

This will only be after the desire for show and fame and name have faded out and you are on the highway of life, speaking the word, not for praise but because you cannot help speak of Me, the inner Lord. You will not go about healing but will go about recognizing the living Word and calling it into expression. The moment it is recognized by you, it will make itself manifest. But if you enter into a state or city (consciousness) where the Word is not received and argument is offered, shake the dust of this dead belief off of you and go your way. It is the dusty, dead argument of these who have to stay behind and bury their dead fathers. All human reasoning belongs to that category.

Inspiration cannot be narrowed into the limitations of human intellect. "Eyes have not seen, ears have not heard, neither hath it entered into the heart of man, the things which are prepared" for them that love the law. If the eyes have not seen and ears have not heard, then why should you listen to the limiting beliefs of the human thought about the coming of your good into manifestation? Do you not see that only when a seal is put on your lips, and you go within to the Me of You and identify yourself with this, can you taste of the glories of the Kingdom. What matter what a thousand books say? What matter what a thousand sermons preach? You have entered into a reality where, having eyes, ye see, and ears, ye hear, that which the limited human sight and hearing is incapable of experiencing. You will flee then from the man whose breath is in his nostrils, who is still trying to sell you his John Smith brand of truth, who is forever talking about the healings he has made or experienced: for you will be in a place where there is nothing to heal—there is only revelation to be brought out. You shall be silent and serene and joyous; a song will be singing deep in your heart that the world cannot help but see. Yea, they shall see the song and say, "You are a celestial being having a happy mask."

Then will you know that the king can play the beggar, but the poor beggar can never possibly play the king. Then will you see the unlimited possibilities of the Son of the living God and will not think it strange that you begin the appropriation of your good; nothing shall be impossible to you.

Do you hear? Do you hear? Do you hear? Nothing is impossible to Me, the Christ. Everything is impossible to me, John Smith. If you still have to drag the corpse of the John Smith and his history of sin and limitations with you, you cannot enter, for you are now a new creature in a new universe, not an old creature patched up. Do you hear? Do you hear?

Be still. It is well. Well. *I* am here—My name is Wonderful. Call upon Me and *I* will answer you. *I* am everywhere evenly present, in the lowest dive of your human belief as well as the most lofty temple. *I* have but to be recognized to be made manifest. If you are in hell, there am *I*; call upon Me and *I* will answer. And judge not from the appearances, for these shall pass in a swirl of hypothetical ether. You shall look for the place thereof, and it too shall be gone, for it will be as the ice upon the river when the summer has come—it has been swallowed up in the activity of the flowing, life-giving river.

Nothing shall be lost, but all shall be saved. Right where you stand is holy ground. The desert you inhabit is full of promise. You do not need to go into a far country; your Father is right where you are, but you have to arise—to recognize His presence and go to Him in consciousness to receive the All-Good, even though you have already wasted it all. You are never hopeless, forlorn, or deserted. You are the Son of the living God, now and here, and you are being Self-revealed. It is wonderful, it is wonderful, it is wonderful.

A new door opens before you. The old things pass away; the binding history of your past has melted into oblivion, and you stand Self-revealed—Son of the living God, with the truth written in your heart. "With God nothing is impossible"—with God-Consciousness—and you have this, as Jesus showed he had it, by recognizing its presence and using it—not with fear and wonder but with boldness and joy; not by thinking that he was a special, favored manifestation of the creation but by accepting the good, the joy, and the power as natural, easy, and free. When will you arise and go unto your Father—cease from the man "whose breath is in his nostrils" and stop this wandering back and forth in the desert of human beliefs and teaching? Within lies the All—the Father.

I will speak to you out of the books of the world and through the men of the world. Fear not—it is well. No sooner are you willing and ready than *I* will supply the avenue through which shall pour forth such new wisdom and revelation that you will wonder; you will be filled with wonder. You will know that it is wonderful, that a new state has been won which is full of the magic of new revelation. Life shall become One, all One—not two but

One, the whole, and you, as a point of consciousness, drawing upon the infinite storehouse of the *All*.

Things that cannot be written shall be told thee; things that cannot be said shall be given thee through the feeling, the wordless feeling. Things that cannot be seen shall be shown thee, and thou shalt know that the old order changeth and that thou art actually standing in the eternal ways. Thou shalt draw from this great eternity everything which thy heart desires—not for selfish consumption, for personal gain and self-aggrandizement, but for the Selfish consumption (the consumption of the real Self) and for the Personal (the divine Self) gain, and for Self (the Son of God-Self) aggrandizement.

> Thoughts come streaming in at their best. Whence and how I know not—cannot make out ... Then it [the composition] keeps on growing, and I keep on expanding it and making it more distinct, and the thing, however long it be, becomes, indeed, almost finished in my head, so that I can afterwards survey it in spirit like a beautiful picture or a fine person, and also hear it in imagination—not indeed successively, as bye and bye it must come out, but as altogether. That is a delight! All the invention and construction go on in me as in a fine strong dream. But the overhearing it all at once is still the best (Mozart).

As the great Mozart conceived his whole composition before he even heard a note, heard it all at once—not note by note, but the total effect of the all—so will you express Me; so will you find that whatsoever the desire be, the expression is as sudden as is the reflection in the mirror when you pass in front of it, and as easy and as perfect and as free from personal effort. You shall find the deep things within yourself and know that the things which "eye hath not seen" are the things which dazzle the human thought beyond all measure.

The gift is not, then, so trivial that it amounts to a little prattling about the words of Jesus or of making a few healings on the earth-plane; it is the eternal going from mansion to mansion, from one glorious expression to another, in the universal consciousness. Thus will you understand how it was that *I*, through the man Jesus, caused many things to happen of which the world has never ceased to talk. Likewise, to you *I* shall reveal things which will cause the doors of the palace of the kings of the earth to fly open to you, and which will finally cause the kings of the earth to seek you out and lay their gifts at your feet.

What is this puny sense interpretation of Me which offers a way to treat and heal disease and to prosper a man? Can it be the anti-Christ, which offers My robe for sale to a lot of dirty gamblers? What do you want with the truth? To be known of men? To set up a new system? To get the applause of the world and have them say of you, "He is a holy man"? What went ye out to see? That which you no doubt found yourself, human or divine, out-pictured everywhere. What do you see but an infinite self-division—good, bad, or indifferent? What went ye out to see? A world full of evil and hatred, sin and disease, that you, poor puny creature, went forth to dope up and set right. Perhaps ye go forth to be a martyr to the cause of Me! Have *I* ever made this demand? And after your self-imposed martyrdom, did you not find out that it was for self-glorification?

When shall you go forth as the Son of the living God—the Bright Messenger with light which automatically dispels darkness? Not because it recognizes darkness as something to get rid of, but because it exists no longer as a reality at the coming of light. What do you bring with you when you go forth into the universe?

My name is Wonderful. *I* sit in the beggar's hut with the riches of the universe hidden away under the rags of the beggar, but *I* am unrecognized. Everyone that looks at Me either turns away or says, "Poor creature! Here, take this penny and buy yourself a crust of bread." But one comes and says, "Wonderful," and *I* answer, "Yea, yea" and rise, transformed from rags to silken garments, with purple and fine linen, with the silken tassels of my purse bursting because of their inability to hold the substance which is there.

My name is Wonderful. *I* lie within the sick, the dumb, the blind, the maimed, awaiting recognition. *I* lie there, a perfect flood of vitality, a stream of consciousness which sees without eyes, hears without ears, speaks without words, and senses a vitality which knows no limitations. *I* am greater than any instrument through which *I* express. *I* await recognition so that the silly garments which have been hung upon Me shall be cast aside and a new, beautiful body shall be made to appear. *I* await the one who will come and say, "It is wonderful" instead of the one who comes in pity and sympathy.

I await the one who will recognize Me in the hell of this physical limitation and this blinding pain of the belief-world, and call Me by name to rise up and cause the lame to go his way leaping for joy, the blind to see, the dumb to sing, the crooked to be made straight, and the dead to arise. *I* await recognition of Me—*I* await the command "Rise up and walk," which follows the recognition. *I* await the command "Open your eyes," to cause sightless eyes to be full of light.

That one who hath the single eye shall perceive Me in the most wretched costume that human belief has put upon Me and shall call Me out by this glorious recognition. *I* await the command "Be whole." Not be made whole, but be that which you eternally are. Who shall recognize Me? Who shall be the unafraid? That one shall tread upon the serpents of belief and the dragons of human sense, and nothing shall by any means hurt him.

Who are you—you who read this page, you who hold this book? *I* speak to you alone, alone, alone. Listen … listen within … within … deep within. Who are you!

If you have heard Me speaking to you, then a great cloud of joy surrounds you, and the peace which passeth all is yours; you know that, irrespective of appearances, everything is all right … peace, peace, peace, peace. It is wonderful. A seal is placed upon your lips. See that you tell no man.

Chapter VII

The Spirit of the Consciousness

"The Spirit of the Consciousness of the
Presence of God is the Source of all Supply."

The Spirit moving "upon the face of the water"—the Spirit of the consciousness is that activating motive which brings into manifestation the unseen things of the spiritual world. The Word becomes flesh by reason of the eternal action of the Spirit. The quickening Spirit is that which has brought it into manifestation here and now.

All people have in some degree the consciousness of the Presence of God. Many can speak volumes of words of and about this consciousness, without manifestation enough to sustain them. Ten thousand holy men, under ten thousand banyan trees, are not able to do what one simple soul, without name or station, can do through the recognition of the Spirit of the Consciousness. Thousands may sit in meditation, in a perfect state of inward bliss, while the worms unfasten the very temple. They may proclaim "Lord, Lord" until the end of time and may experience all sorts of Nirvana while their bodies are rotting with disease, yet until the Spirit becomes flesh, It remains invisible; hence, as far as the human manifestation is concerned, useless and unreal.

What though I tell you of the riches of my Father, the King, if I drop with hunger while relating the fabulous stories? What though I tell you of the all-health of Spirit, if I die with disease as I am speaking? What though I tell you of the guiding influence of Spirit, if I cling tenaciously to a position, looking to an organization or a salary to support my feeble voice, while I loudly proclaim, "The Lord is the source of my supply"?

Until recognition of the Spirit—the living, pulsating Spirit of the Presence of the Consciousness of God—is made, man is but another fully equipped power station, with infinite possibilities to illuminate the whole universe but with no manifestation. As a beautifully installed system of electricity remains in darkness until the wires are connected, so man, though he be fully equipped to flood his universe with light, remains in darkness until he recognizes the presence of the Spirit.

We recognize that the universe is filled with infinite music, which may be produced anywhere at any time yet is inaudible until this recognition. So likewise we shall come to realize the All-Presence of God, and this recognition in the *All-Now* will produce the quickening Spirit of instantaneous accomplishment.

Hitherto we have thought of music as stored up in a gramophone record or in the soul of a person. We had no thought of its All-Presence in the *All-Now* but had to go to people and localities to produce it. However wonderful the manifestation was, it was always hedged about with limitations. Then suddenly came the recognition of the All-Presence in the *All-Now*, and at that instant it became known that it was possible anywhere, at any time, instead of in a single isolated spot. So when man comes to recognize the Spirit of the Consciousness, he realizes that instead of this magnificent power being stored up in certain spiritual teachers, books, or places, it is infinite and is instantly available in an intensely practical way.

"If the blind lead the blind, both shall fall into the ditch." The Truth-speaker will be known by the impersonality of his words. He will not speak of himself but of the power that has sent him into expression. He will not spread himself as a peacock or call attention to his high spiritual accomplishments. "What went ye out to see?" When are you going to see Me, the glorious Spirit of the Consciousness of the Presence of God in the midst of *You*?

To the coward, death comes many times. "Prove Me and see" is the command. "By their works"—not by their words—"shall ye know them." "Where the Spirit of the Lord is, there is liberty," there is the multitude listening. Look about you and see—the living, pulsating, vibrating Spirit of the Consciousness, the glorious thing made alive. A thousand wonderful buildings dedicated to God and His work stand empty while words of, and about, the truth are poured out in many tomes. Once the Spirit of the Consciousness of the Presence of God enters in, the walls of the churches will burst with the multitude. Such a power is the Light that leads, by an invisible way, the souls that seek the Light. And this glorious manifestation is possible to you. You—do you hear?

You will lay aside the filthy garments of personal worship; you will flee from man "whose breath is in his nostrils." You will cease the worship of personality, however consecrated and holy it may appear. You will thrill with the Spirit which is at last recognized within you. You will know that "it is well" with Me.

As the Spirit of the Consciousness of the Presence of God is recognized within you, the belief of poverty or limitation of any sort evaporates. As the mist of belief clears away, you find the kingdom of heaven here and now. This recognition of the Spirit of the Consciousness of the Presence of God acts not as a destroyer of evil but as a revelator of the All-Good in the All-Now and instantly brings out the reality: "Whereas I was blind, now I see." When it is once *now* to the soul, it has *always* been *now*.

As you are reading these lines, *I*, the Spirit of the Consciousness of the Presence, am awaiting recognition. You—yes, you, the poor little discounted one, the one who stood farthest from the pulpit and received scarcely a sign of recognition from the consecrated souls—*I* have come to you, and *I* am the same One who has been standing at the door of your consciousness knocking for ages.

"Behold, I (the Spirit) stand at the door (of your consciousness) and knock. If any (no distinction is made) man … open the door, I will come in to him, and sup with him, and he with me"—no matter who you are, neither the grade nor the length of your teaching nor the fears of condemnation.

You who read this page, do you hear? Do you see? *I* am that which will tear the veil of belief, and you shall see, not a little demonstration of supply that will last you for a week but the fields white with substance, and you shall know that deep in the secret place of your being is the key to the Universe. The catering to persons will drop away. You will ask no man permission to perform the work *I* sent you to perform. Those that are for thee are more than those that are against thee, for there is but One, the Only, the All.

It is the *recognition* of the Spirit of the Consciousness of the Presence of God that suddenly transforms you and your universe, just as the spirit of the dance transforms an inert figure to a flying, moving thing of grace. Just as a smile transforms the entire face of a person, so the recognition of the Spirit will transform, with all the ease and none of the difficulties of human effort, the entire life of a person. "The fashion of his countenance was changed." Do you hear, you who read this page, how radical the change is? The "fashion," even the hard lines that have been with you so long, whether in body, in expression, or accomplishment, all are subject to change to the extent that you will know "the former things have passed away.

Beloved, do you see the extent of this glorious awakening? Do you see the sublime heights to which the Spirit of the Consciousness shall lead you? Not a little healing for the moment, but the revelation of the Son of the living God here and now, and this revelation will naturally change the "fashion" of your entire expression.

What the Spirit of the Consciousness of the Presence of God "decrees," that shall come to pass, for it is merely decreeing the manifestations it sees in the kingdom. All the human laws fade into nothingness as shadows disappear before the light. Every law is turned aside in order that the real lasting Grace of the living Word shall be made manifest. Why will you bring such limited measures to the fount of the All-Present?

When will you stop trying to do things and appropriate the All-Presence? Only when you have recognized the Spirit of the Consciousness of the Presence of God. Only when you stop running to and fro, asking people and listening to people whose breath is in their nostrils. *I* break the bread with you. "Give not that which is holy unto dogs." Why will you argue and compare and listen to some wisehead hash and rehash the wondrous words that *I* speak direct to you from my Son? Be still ... be still. "Thou fool, do you not know that a seed must first fall into the ground before it can be made alive?" When are you going to let the stillness hold you in its heavenly bonds of secrecy and revelation—Self-revelation—My interpretation to you, to you alone?

The Spirit of the Consciousness of the Presence of God is the source of all supply. Not of *some* supply, but of all supply. When you know this, you will not try to hoard; there will be no need, for supply will be as much present in one locality as another. It will be wherever you are and wherever you desire it. Do you hear? You who read this page? Look between the lines; *I* speak to you. *I* cast not my pearls before swine, but *I* am pouring them out to you. *I* am giving you the keys to the gates of heaven, which you have sought through many avenues and not yet found. The sordid robes of personality, name, and fame will fall finally from you, and you shall put on the glorious, shimmering robes of immortality. *I* speak to you. Do you hear? You who read this page?

When you are ready to lay down your life, then shall you find it. Then you shall find that you are alive for the first time, and instead of the ghastly futility of trying to get enough health, happiness, and supply to live by, you will find yourself in the Presence of the All, where nothing is lacking.

That Power which you tried to produce so that you might be known of men shall be so innately interwoven into your soul that it will be a natural manifestation. Heretofore you have said your words and done your deeds to be known of the populace. You wanted always to be sure that your name was attached to any healing or help that was given. Then "through a glass, darkly," but now "face to face"—face to face with the power you have sought for so long.

When you are once enveloped in the secrecy of the Spirit of the Presence, you will know why it is that "their shoes wax not old" and that the "manna falls daily."

"The whole creation groaneth ... to wit, for the redemption of the body." We see this redemption within ourselves. Verily this has been true to our blinded eyes. A world of people writhing and twisting, begging for mercy, seeking money, health, success, happiness—eternally seeking "things" and finding only ashes. The veil shall be torn from your eyes by the Spirit of the Consciousness of the Presence of God, and you shall see that the whole creation—your creation, your heaven—rejoiceth and maketh a glad sound, for the Redeemer has come into manifestation. Do you see? You who read this page? You?

You may call Me by a thousand names, yet *I* am One. *"You are not another, but the same One"* will finally be said of you. You will realize that you are not a separate little manifestation, with certain powers stored up within you, but you are the same One. There is only the One. It is One ... It is Won ... It is Wonderful. The limitations of human language make it almost impossible to express anything but the vaguest idea of this glorious revelation. "Behold, I make all things new"—*I*, the Spirit of the Consciousness. *I* make them new to the eyes that have been seeing through the belief of birth, growth, maturity, decay. *I* make them new by revelation of the eternal freshness and newness of the changeless universe of God. *I* make you new by revealing your true self to you. The quickening Spirit of the Presence brings into manifestation power hitherto unknown.

Dare you go your way with Me alone? Dare you rely on Me, the Spirit? Dare you to launch out into deep waters and push out the borders of your tent? You—*I* speak to you, who read this page!

Be still, then—*I am here now*. *I* am the Spirit of the Consciousness. You have always had the Consciousness of the Presence of God, no matter how little you knew it, no matter how many spiritual busybodies have told you that it has to be evolved. If you were created by God and out of God, you have had the consciousness of God always, and no lying mortal man, no matter if he have a thousand diplomas to tell of his learning, shall make this false. You have this Consciousness, whether someone has told you you were consecrated or damned. You are the Son of the living God, and you are already in possession of this Consciousness, and when you recognize the Spirit of the Consciousness, the instantaneous manifestation of the kingdom is revealed to you.

Do not look for a sign. *I*, the I AM, descend into the stagnant pool of your human belief. *I* descend into the dirty waters and purify them. *I* free you from the prison of your own making.

The Spirit of the Consciousness of the Presence of God is the Source of all Supply—the overflowing, unending, unlimited source of all supply. "I come quickly." "In the twinkling of an eye" all—not some, but all—shall be changed.

The Spirit of the Consciousness of the Presence of God is the Source of all Supply. I thank you, Father.

Chapter VIII

Prayer and Poison

In a newspaper recently appeared a report of a plague of grasshoppers, which were said to be destroying all the crops in a certain part of the States. A mass meeting was held, and prayers for deliverance were offered up. Quoting from a New York paper of July 28th, 1931:

> Prayers and poison were resorted to as weapons. More than a thousand farmers knelt and asked divine aid against the scourge.

They prayed and then resorted to poison. There is no condemnation in mentioning this article. It is only a trite illustration of how many people pray and what they think of the power to which they pray. They pray and then resort to the use of poison to deliver them. They treat in the most approved manner and then resort to all sorts of means to make things happen. They plant and then immediately dig up the seed to see if anything has taken place. They place an egg under the hen and then crack it open to ascertain if anything has transpired.

"O ye of little faith," why do you look for a sign? Why do you pray to a tribal god when the way of true prayer is open to you, and the way of sure success? Why will you doubt? Why will you pray and then resort to poison? Know ye not that "my ways are not your ways? My ways are as high above your ways as the heavens are above the earth."

Have *I* not said unto you, "If ye have faith as a grain of mustard seed, ye shall say unto this mountain, remove hence to yonder place; and it shall remove." *I* did not suggest the ways and means of bringing it to pass after you had spoken the word. Have *I* not told you, "Thy faith hath made thee whole"? Not *nearly* whole, but whole.

If you would only take your attention away from the mountain of difficulties that has been in your way all these years, it would then be possible for your troubles to disappear. Then would you be able to say, with a thrill of joy, "This is the Lord's doings. It is marvelous in our eyes."

Ask of Me, and *I* will show you things that are not written in any book:

> The hills melted like wax at the presence of the Lord, at the presence of the Lord of the whole earth (Ps. 97:5).

There is nothing which can stand before the presence of this unconditioned Power. The most adamant condition you can conceive of melts like so much wax in the fierce heat of a furnace. What is the condition that you hug to yourself as difficult and impossible of destruction? In the presence of the unconditioned Power, nothing is a condition—nothing is difficult, nothing is impossible, and this presence is the Lord which is in the midst of thee, *now* and always.

Do you see what the power of God is? "Be not afraid; it is I." I AM—not the little god built up by a man or a nation but I AM THAT I AM—and *I* am here *now* to deliver you—yes, you who read this line—out of the hand of your oppressor, whatever and whoever he may be.

"Open thou my eyes, that I may behold the wondrous things of the Lord" is the new prayer that fills your heart, for it is the prayer that asks to see that which is already created and not the prayer that attempts to create or thinks to win a special favor from a tribal god.

> Open thou mine eyes, that I may behold the wondrous things of the Lord (Ps. 119:8).

> Make a joyous noise unto the Lord, all ye lands. Serve the Lord with gladness: come before his presence with singing. Know ye that the Lord he is

God: it is he that hath made us, and not we ourselves; we are his people, and the sheep of his pasture. Enter into his gates with thanksgiving, and into his courts with praise: be thankful unto him, and bless his name. For the Lord is good; his mercy is everlasting and his truth endureth to all generations (Ps. 100:1-5).

The making of a joyous noise will take place when you realize the presence of God and worship Him in Spirit and in truth, instead of paying tribute to a tribal god that sits upon a throne judging the sinners of the earth. Do you see the wondrous things that are to be revealed to you, the Son of the living God?

Thy hands have made me and fashioned me: give me understanding, that I may learn thy commandments (Ps. 119:73).

If for one instant you realize the magnificent truth which lies back of the statement "Thy hands have made me and fashioned me," you will see that the hand of the Potter did not shake, nor was Its work distorted and full of disease and limitations.

Look unto me, all the ends of the earth, and be ye saved (Isa. 45:22).

Saved from the terrible fury of the misguided beliefs which have run wild and gone prodigal in their search after things.

Thy testimonies are wonderful; therefore doth my soul keep them (Ps. 119:129).

The testimonies of the Lord are wonderful—and you will awaken to this glorious truth and go about in your universe calling the name of "Wonderful" down upon everything. The ugly shell shall break and give forth its promise at the calling of its name; the soul of the hard, parched earth shall answer and give forth her abundance of flowers and fruits; your forty years wandering in the desert of human thought shall come to an end, and you shall see that you have been going around in circles, in a desert of your own making.

> The entrance of thy word giveth light; it giveth understanding unto the simple (Ps. 119:130).

Do you hear? The entrance of the word giveth light. Speak the *Word*, then, and see the illumination take place. See that the deaf hear, the blind see, the lame walk; come again unto Me and tell Me. "Even the devils are subject unto you"—the devils of belief. Can you see? Can you hear?

> Now we know that what things soever the law saith, it saith to them who are under the law: that every mouth may be stopped, and all the world may become guilty before God (Rom. 3:19).

The doctrine that man is a worm of the dust and a sinner conceived in sin is found herein stated. But between the lines lie the glorious pearls of truth. It saith to them who are under the law: "If ye are led by the Spirit, ye are not under the law"—you are freed from the human law of destiny and fate which hangs like an ugly black cloud over mankind and from which you cannot escape so long as you are *under* the human law.

Presently you see that the law of human belief is put to naught and you are no more under it; you are under grace.

> But now the righteousness of God without the law is manifested, being witnessed by the law and the prophets (Rom. 3:21).

Do you note that the righteousness *without* the law is made manifest? Everything that Jesus did in his wondrous career was "without the law"—without the laws of the human reasoning or of the best of the accepted laws of physics of that day or any other day.

> And they shall sit every man under his vine and under his fig tree; and none shall make them afraid: for the mouth of the Lord of hosts has spoken it (Mic. 4:4).

Beloved, you are gradually coming into your divine inheritance; you shall see the wonders of the new heaven and the new earth.

Behold, all they that were incensed against thee shall be ashamed and confounded: they shall be as nothing; and they that strive with thee shall perish (Isa. 41:11).

The host of evil thoughts that have seemingly tried to destroy you, no matter from what source, shall be confounded and shall be as nothing; one by one, as these thoughts come forth to strive with you, the Son of the living God, they shall perish. It is wonderful.

Fear them not; for I am with thee: be not dismayed; for I am thy God. I will strengthen thee; yea, I will help thee; yea, I will uphold thee with the right hand of my righteousness (Isa. 41:10).

If ye be upheld by the right hand of My righteousness, ye have nothing to fear. Therefore, beloved, when ye pray, do not resort to poison. Stand and see the salvation from the plague of evil thoughts and beliefs that is destroying your substance.

Chapter IX

O Ye of Little Faith

One of the most glorious things said by the Master was "O ye of little faith," addressed to the disciples after they had failed to heal the sick child. It is glorious because unless the Master had known that it lay perfectly within the power of the disciples to have brought forth this healing, he would not have rebuked them for their failure. Do you see, then, how the secret doctrine is hidden away for those who have eyes? Do you see that you are never rebuked for having left undone something that you could not do? In the rebuke, the powerful encouragement comes that it was, and still is, within the scope of your possibility to perform that which you failed to do.

"Be of good cheer: I (the I AM) have overcome the world." "*I* have *come over* the world" would give a more adequate idea, for with the coming of the Christ into manifestation, the difficulties of human belief are set aside.

"His rebuke was terrible." It is terrible because it always carries with it the fact that the one rebuked could have fulfilled perfectly that which was before him to do. Even in the midst of the consuming fire of the rebuke, there comes that recognition that unless you had been fully able to perform the task, you would not have been rebuked for having left it undone.

A glorious something comes out of it all: the recognition that, even though you failed, still you had the power to do the thing which seemed impossible, and this is why you shall understand the saying "the chastening of the Lord is sweet"—sweet, as a doctor might speak of a bitter drug being sweet because of what it contained, not by reason of its flavor.

"Whom the Lord loveth he chasteneth." No one wastes any time correcting a fool. His mistakes are set down to natural incapacity. The servant who is fully capable of performing the task is rebuked if he fails, and in the stinging rebuke, the master really shows forth his love. He shows forth his recognition of the power being present in the one who has been rebuked. The wise servant is not, then, turned awry by a rebuke; he spends no time nursing a feeling of injustice, but instantly causes the prickly chestnut burr of rebuke to reveal the food inside.

In every rebuke administered to you, there lies the glorious recognition of the fact that within you is the power to perform perfectly that which you failed to do. A rebuke, when handled from this elevation, should be as a burst of light to you—a new door swinging open, a new opportunity to make your agreement with the power to accomplish that which you previously failed to perform.

Jesus' rebuke to the disciples, "O ye of little faith," was only saying in so many words, "I recognize within you the perfect capacity to have brought this healing into manifestation." Despise not, then, the chastening of the Lord."

"Prove me and see" is the eternal command. As soon as a new scope of understanding comes to the individual, he must put it into practice, and if he is willing and ready to do this, he will not merit the rebuke. Perhaps he will only see the rebuke and will nurse it as a seeming injustice. Perhaps he will say he was doing the best he could. You will never be rebuked unless you have failed to do that which was possible for you to do.

Therefore rejoice. One moment's consciousness of this will help to clear away much underbrush from the forest of life. You will be able to destroy many old plague-spots which have been clinging to you. You have tried every means possible to drain the ugly swamps of resentment caused by some rebuke in the past, but always they remained, and at the slightest provocation they were full of stagnant waters again. There is no getting rid of the sting of rebuke unless you see that within it is the sincerest and greatest acknowledgment of your power to accomplish that which you failed to do.

A new joy will come to you. "Even the devils are subject unto us." Even the devilish thoughts that have stayed to torment us for years suddenly give way. We have learned the manner in which the beast is transformed into the prince. We have discovered why we can say of the evil appearances, "It is wonderful." We see literally why, if we make our bed in hell, God is there. Looking through appearances, we see and recognize the Power. The fiercer the rebuke the greater the recognition of the Power. "Whom the Lord loveth he chasteneth" might be quoted as "Whom the Lord loveth he calls attention always to the wonderful power within them which they failed to employ."

"Arise, arise, get thee up into a high place. Get thee up to the Mount of Revelation. See the old sores of resentment and hurt healed and vanished by the glorious recognition of what is back of them.

Enter into your temple and cleanse it of all the thieves, dove sellers, and moneychangers. Whip out the robbers that steal your peace and joy. Destroy the mental bookkeeper of past evils. Overturn the tables of the moneychangers who are forever trying to sell the precious word of life. The doves of purity are freed, not sold. The glory of the soul stands revealed.

The wrath of man shall bless thee because it will only be an indirect way of telling and pointing out to you the fact that you failed unnecessarily. Then will come the glorious recognition that even they, your enemies, recognize that you had the power within you possible of accomplishment, only you failed to use it.

Fear not. It is I.

Chapter X

Blessings

*They were gathered together in one
place, of their own accord, and were
baptized of the Holy Ghost.*

Many people do not accept the blessing of the fulfillment of the law. Time after time, they are gathered together of their own accord, but by failing to recognize that they have functioned a law that is fruitful of results, they sit trying to make the goodness of God appear instead of receiving the baptism of the Holy Ghost; instead of feeling the down-pouring floods of light and illumination—the great engulfing inrush of blessings. To function the law of Spirit is to automatically release Its fulfillment.

Awake, thou that sleepest—awake and arise from the dead—and Christ, your inner Lord, shall give thee light; you shall suddenly and with great happiness of soul make a joyful noise unto the Lord, for you will see and hear great floods of blessings, blessings so numerous they are as the sands of the sea.

Right here and now, right throughout the blackness of your material thinking, break the floods of light that reveal the blessings as already here and now. As the coming of light in a darkened art gallery reveals thousands of treasures which were there all the time yet invisible, so the coming of your recognition of the Presence illumes your very own universe and reveals to you the infinite blessings all about you.

"Blessings, blessings, blessings, so many you cannot count them." Right now, right here—because you and I have met at this place of at-one-ment. You, the reader, and I,

the writer, have met in this place of glorious recognition of the inner Christ. We have done this of our accord. We are at this glorious instant functioning the baptism of the Holy Ghost. Yes, you are at this instant baptized by the Holy Ghost, the great flood of light which reveals heaven—here and now. At this instant, your eyes are being bathed in pure light, and the scales of human reasoning and limitation are dropping from them. You are at this instant seeing the wonders of the kingdom here and now. You are filled with the thrilling sense of joy, and you exclaim for the first time in your life, "Blessings, blessings, blessings—so many you cannot count them."

You exclaim from the heights of recognition the vision that is revealed to you of your true Self. Blessings, blessings, blessings. They are at this instant flooding you. You are clear and free from the limitations of former beliefs. You lave in the glorious waters of Spirit. A million barnacles of belief fall from you. Your entire being—your body, with your whole universe—is permeated with the pure, glistening, pulsating substance of Life, Life of God. And you, standing in the eternal ways, are experiencing this oneness with the universal Whole—the result of having recognized that you have functioned a definite law of Spirit. Do you see? Are you at this instant experiencing the baptism which you have brought about? You who read this page?

Phrases and words are old and trite. Repeating the wondrous words of the Bible is like stating so many platitudes to ears that hear only the letter, or like the remembrance of so many tormenting, unfulfilled promises to those who are trying to make these words come true. Attempting to record the inspiration of the Almighty in manmade words is almost impossible. No wonder, then, that the Spirit says, "I am the voice of the one crying in the wilderness" (of human hope) … "prepare ye the way of our Lord." The way of our Lord is the way that is flooded with blessings. It is the way of Self-expression, the way of the Christ-Self. It is a way that comes not with reason, but is *impressed* upon the mind, as a man who has lain down to sleep in a dark night finds that, while he slept, the new day has already burst upon him—unannounced, unheralded.

Who can stay the dawn? No more can you withstay the glorious dawn of the kingdom of heaven that even now is breaking over the horizon of your night of self-imposed limitations and tears. Even now, you stand at the threshold of a new day, which is the day of *Now*, the Day of Revelation—you who read this page, do you hear? It is *daybreak* for you. Do you hear? The hard, ugly objects against which you stumbled in the darkness are revealed in the light of truth as glorious blessings.

The kingdom of heaven is not far off—it is near. Awake! It is for your acceptance. Too good to be true? Yes, to the human sense. Must take time? Yes, to the human sense. Is not practical? Not to the human sense. A thousand have tried it and failed, just because they *tried* it. There is no effort in the action of God. Unlabored, untrammeled, free into expression is its manner of appearing. "Ten thousand shall fall at thy right hand, but it shall not come nigh thee." Believest thou this?

The object in the distance does not grow in size as you move towards it, although it seems to. It has always been the same size, but as you approach it, it appears to be larger than when viewed from afar. So with the kingdom, which you perceive in the far distance of your life. Nothing can be added to it, nothing taken away from it. You are playing with the shadows of belief when you think to add or take from the word of God. You cannot take a little of the substance of God's riches as a thief might steal a handful of money from a bank. There is no separation and no place to take anything *from*. Everything is here and now. You cannot take anything from the sum total of a radio concert; regardless of the size of the room into which it is released, it is inside, outside, everywhere, and inseparably joined all the time. It is only the limited human concept that stops the concert at one point and starts it the other side of a wall. In reality it is everywhere and complete.

You do not grow into the kingdom, yet to the human sense of things you *seem* to be growing more and more spiritual. What you *are* doing is becoming more and more aware of the kingdom as here and now. Healing, then, is only becoming aware, in a more or less degree, of a spiritually perfect man. Do you not take heart at the glorious news that the kingdom is already here and lay aside the sin of trying to make it appear, or trying to keep others out of the glorious possibilities of the Sons of the living God, by first telling them they are sons of perdition and are full of evil? Awake, thou that sleepest! When will you cease the condemnation of My kingdom? When will you cease the stone casting at yourself and others? "Neither do I condemn thee: go, and sin no more."

Blessings, blessings, blessings. So many you cannot count them. Not the old concept of blessings, which is a cross between self-pity and self-righteousness, but the revelation of the Kingdom. When the word *blessings* is said from the vantage point of recognition, it actually floods the soul with light and glory. Speak the word. "Only speak the word, and my servant (body) shall be healed," and the word is: "I will. Bless you, bless you, bless you."

Blessings, blessings, blessings go out from this state of consciousness like millions of birds loosed on a plague-ridden country. Each one shall destroy the ugly pest from off the land, and in a twinkling of an eye, you shall see the land (your land) green and fresh and fair. Blessings, blessings, blessings. "My word ... shall not return unto me void, but it shall accomplish that which I please, and it shall prosper in the thing whereunto I sent it." Do you hear? You who read this page? You? "And it shall come to pass (do you hear? This is a statement of fact; it shall come to pass! It is bound to happen) if thou shalt hearken diligently unto the voice of thy Lord (not the voice of man) ... that the Lord thy God (the Lord in the midst of thee) will set thee on high above all nations of the earth"—above all the false law that you have functioned under on the earth.

"And all these blessings shall come on thee, and overtake thee." Beloved, put up your sword. Do you not see that, even while you are fighting in the darkness, these blessings are finally bound to overtake thee? They shall come upon thee like a thief in the night. A thief in the night comes in silence, at the darkest hour.

Be still ... be still ... be still. It is well with thee. "Blessed shalt thou be in the city and blessed shalt thou be in the field." Wherever thou art, thou shalt see the floods of blessings about thee. Whether it be in the city or whether it be in the open field, the All-Blessing is there. There is no place where the I AM, with Its full quota of blessings, is not.

Do you see, then, why the command is "Go, take no thought for the scrip, the purse, the robe, the ring, the journey"? But as long as man is still working on the personal plane, he finds his mind much occupied with the amassing of things for the journey. He says, "I want much money, so that I can do the work of God and help others." Tear off this mask of selfishness and stand free. If you want much, it is to be known of man and your charities. The Son of the living God does not want much, knowing that he has it all. He has nothing to do with possessions but to give them away. He must of necessity break the bread in order that the multitudes may be filled. Be still ... be still ... be still. That which is obvious does not need to be mentioned.

"Blessed shall be the fruit of thy body, and the fruit of thy ground, and the fruit of thy cattle, the increase of thy kine, and the flocks of thy sheep." Everything you touch will be blessed, and the glorious universe which seemed for lo these many years to be a desert, parched and dried, will suddenly burst into bloom, and everything shall be blessed and glorified, while the beautiful fruits of the former desert shall be unlimited.

Do you see, beloved? The eleventh hour has struck, and floods of light are emanating from the very presence of the Kingdom here and now, filtering through the darkness of your human belief,

"Blessed shall be thy basket and thy store." Blessed shall be the increase of good that shall fill every empty place of former years, and thou shalt be the impersonal giver of all good, learning that the way of revelation of increase lies in the ability to place yourself in the role of the infinite, impersonal giver.

The world is flooding over with joy. running over with the glory of this infinite downpour of blessings that you have called forth by recognition. If you lie in a bed racked with pain, the streaming light of this blessing will reveal to your human eye the perfection of the Son of the living God, and you shall arise. Do you hear? If you sit in rags, wondering where the next meal is coming from, you shall suddenly find yourself richly clothed and know the abundance of the child of the Highest. Do you hear? Do you hear, you who read this line? Do you see that whereas before, you were blind, but now you can see—*Now*. Do you utter silently, "Blessings, blessings, blessings—so many you cannot count them"? Do you?

And whithersoever thou goest, thou shalt find. "Blessed shalt thou be when thou goest in, and blessed shalt thou be when thou goest out" … "Be not afraid; it is I." Be not afraid of your good—*I* give the kingdom of heaven not to the adult but to the child. The child can accept its world and heaven of blessings without question, without reason, without tiresome argument or trying to make it happen. Do you see that the adult is the only one who can commit adultery? He adulterates everything, even the word of God. He places heaven at the end of a human life of misery and makes the gateway thereunto death—whereas *I* am the Life.

The kingdom of heaven shall not be taken by violence, by reason; neither shall it be entered through the portals of death. And yet *you* die daily, and *you* must be born again. You die to the human beliefs of today, no matter how high and fine they seemed to be. You die daily, to be born again to a greater and more beautiful sense of the Presence. You are becoming more and more aware of the Presence, and as you approach it through this awareness, you see it more and more in detail. As descending from the air in a plane you at first see only a small speck, which on closer examination divides and subdivides itself until it is seen as a great and flourishing city, so will the points of truth that you have conceived at a far distance of human thought reveal themselves as great and glorious states of consciousness, and the idea will unfold as you approach this revelation.

After all, beloved, "Ye have not chosen me, but I have chosen you, and ordained you, that ye should go forth and bring forth fruit ... that whatsoever ye shall ask of the Father in my name (nature), he may give it you." A great burst of revelation comes with "ye have not chosen me." All these years, we have thought that we did something personal when we chose to follow after the Master. We were laboring under self-hypnotism that *we* were making a sacrifice, becoming a martyr, or else we were actuated by fear. Suddenly we find that this is all false and that "ye did not choose me, but I have chosen and ordained you." This very Power chose you.

Do you hear, you who read this page, this line? Do you hear that you were chosen—that you were caught in the net of which the Master spoke? "I will make you fishers of men." Caught in the net and chosen for a glorious expression of the blessings of the Kingdom here and now! And further, you were ordained—not by some person or organization; not because someone pronounced certain words and sang songs over you were you ordained, but in spite of this, and in spite of even the condemnation that might have been cast upon you. "I have chosen you, and ordained you, that you should go and bring forth fruit."

Do you hear? You who read this page? You? Do you begin to see why *I* have said unto you, "Be still, and know that I am God." Be still, and know, and listen to what *I* have to say to you.

Dare you sit in this glorious baptism, which is even at this instant going on, and accept the blessing "I have chosen you" and be ready to hear the command "Go into all the world and preach the gospel." Dare you be ready to go into this wretched place in which you lived—your consciousness—and say, "Be of good cheer. It is *I*. Blessings. Blessings. Blessings"? Dare you say to your personal devil, "It is wonderful. Blessings. Blessings. Blessings," knowing that there is only One and that it is *I*? When you recognize Me as there, *I* will transform the darkness into light, and the shadows of human belief shall flee away. It is well. It is wonderful.

Blessings, blessings, blessings. So many you cannot count them. Let that be *impressed* upon your consciousness, and it will express in your daily life.

> Blessings here and blessings there,
> Blessings here and blessings there,
> Blessings here and blessings there,
> Blessings everywhere ...

… shall form itself into a wondrous melody and will go singing through your glorious day like a host of golden butterflies, darting to and fro over a field of sunny flowers.

Blessings, blessings, blessings—
so many you cannot count them.

Chapter XI

At the Feet of the Master

*And they found him clothed, and in his right
mind, sitting at the feet of the Master.*

They found that maniac who had been living in the
tombs, who had torn himself in anguish, who had frightened
others, clothed and in his right mind, sitting at the feet of
the Master.

The story of the maniac is the story of every man. It
is your story. When the Christ passes by, He finds you in
the tombs of the past, dwelling with dead thoughts and
conditions; living with the whited bones of past accomplishments or fears; hiding behind the tombs of personality;
trying to make that which is dead and done with appear to
be alive; screaming to the passerby in a ghastly voice, swollen
with pride and egotism, telling of your attainments. No
wonder, then, when the voice of the Christ is heard, you
call out, "What have we to do with thee? Go away and
leave us alone."

The old personality, with its graveyard full of pride
of personal attainment, fears to give up its only claim to
attention. It has built tombs, elaborate and ornate, to each
of its accomplishments. It has dug deep into the stones,
the records of what it has done, and it hates to see this
passing into the limbo of oblivion.

Many a man has awakened to find himself in this
graveyard, living the life of a maniac, fingering over the
dead things and wondering why life was so uneventful
and ugly. Mentally he lives with the dead. He heeds not
the injunction "let the dead bury their dead." He has his
tombs to which he is bound. There are, in every mental
cemetery, ghastly vaults of ugly things, memories of

failure, disease, and limitation. Their history is scratched deep in the cold marble.

"Follow me; and let the dead bury their dead" must be obeyed implicitly. Nothing in the past is worthy of consideration; nothing that you have done or left undone is worthy of remembrance. "Come out from among them and be ye separate." Come out from the graveyard of your own making; leave every tomb and be free. You give up nothing when you give up the personal idea for the Christ. The new day dawns across the cold marbles of the past, and you awaken to glorious possibilities. The Master speaks to you and says, "It is well."

The dirty rags of personal beliefs and griefs fall away, and you are naked, stripped of your personal impediment. Everything seems to go away, and then you are "clothed" in your right mind (the Christ-Mind), sitting at the feet of the Master (the inner Lord). At last "the peace that passeth all understanding" enfolds you, and you rest. The floods of forgetfulness wash away the debris of yesteryears, and in the place of the tombs are fields of lilies—fields of fresh attainment and glory. You are alive, and the dead thing has been carried out of your life. "Though a man were dead, yet shall he live" has been made literally true for you. The new life that is surging through your being is the life that has left the past forever.

It is reported that when the maniac child was brought to the Master, his parents went into elaborate details of the evil of which he suffered and then said, "If thou possibly can, good Master, heal him." The Master replied: "Why did you say 'possibly'?" Whether this is accurately recorded or not, it brings with it the strident, flaming question: why did you say "possibly"? Why do you, who admit the all-power of God and yourself as the Son of God, wonder whether He can possibly accomplish the trifling thing that you are seeking?

"O ye of little faith" is the rebuke that comes to us time and time again, as we see that we are constantly returning to the cemetery of past failures—looking among the dead bones of yesterday for a spark of life, whitewashing the rotten caskets of yesterday's attainments, trying to make them as new.

Caught in the old beliefs, we recite the evils we have suffered at great length. We go into the ghastly details of past accomplishments. We tell what we have done to the glory of God instead of showing forth the true consciousness of God in the present manifestation.

The Light burns high these days; the coming of the Christ is taking place in many—not through or by some creed, but through the awakening of the "maniac" in the tomb of dead beliefs. "The wisdom of man is foolishness in the eyes of God." Then the man with this wisdom must be insane in the true sense of the word. Inversely speaking, "the wisdom of God is foolishness in the eye of man," and Jesus was accordingly considered a fanatic or insane man. But once the glory of Christ steals upon you and you are ready to "rise and follow me," you will know the peace, the glorious peace that passeth all understanding.

Beloved, you are not giving up anything when you leave the tomb of yesterday; when you leave the graveyard of relative thought and belief. You are coming out into the new dimension, the dimension of infinity, as it were, the place where you begin to see the naturalness of God's love toward you. This love enables you to see clearly beyond the dead beliefs into life eternal.

What a glory comes to you when you find yourself in your right Mind. For the first time, the feeling of assurance comes to you; the consciousness of peace; the beauty of balance and soundness.

Lazarus comes out of his tomb, and the grave clothes of old beliefs are cut away from him. "Ye must be born again." To be born again does not imply a process of making over an old thing. It is a casting off of the old, as it were, and an appropriation of the new. It is a conscious recognition of the agelessness of Spirit in all its glorious manifestation here and now.

Are you the maniac in the tomb? You who read? Have you the tombs of cold marble hidden away in the darkness of your mind? The Master is passing; even now, as you read, *I* am speaking to you. *I* am calling to you to "come out from among them and be separate" Leave all the dead things of the past and come out into the glorious sunshine of today. You are not losing anything by this giving up.

When the maniacal thoughts of relativity are cast from you, they are self-destroyed. They are drowned in the sea of oblivion. They are gone forever. And their name is legion. A thousand little dishonesties and conceits disappear before the searchlight of the New Idea. The coddling and petting of the human personality is cast off as so much excess baggage. You stand revealed and free—the Son of the living God—not asking again "if you possibly can" but rather, accepting the glorious gift of decreeing, of speaking the word. What is so strange and weird about the fact that a universe evolved out of a God-power should be found in full possession of this God-power? What is so magic about the fact that you should find this God-power operating in your life and bringing out the natural results of this power? As we recognize the Presence more and more, we realize that Its manifestation is only natural.

Drink deep, beloved, of the waters of Life—the refreshing sense of joy that comes over you when you realize that you are clothed and in your right mind, sitting at the feet of the Master. It is well. Fear not.

Chapter XII

Revelation

Every man is a teacher after one fashion or another, and many are teachers of the word of Jesus, of Buddha, of Mohammed. All teaching is of and about the subject. It is eternally the letter, dead and cold. Fused with the enthusiasm of the teacher, it becomes alive for the time but lapses again into the dead, cold thing. Hence, thousands today find themselves well-stocked with the letter of truth and yet are unable to make manifest the promises that have so richly been made to man.

"Physician, heal thyself" is the command of Spirit to the teacher. "What hast thou in your house?" is the searching question. The teacher at last learns that if he will teach he must live from his own words; he must eat them, and many times he is unable to do this. He is on an endless treadmill. He traces over and over the same monotonous pattern; he hears himself reiterating the same words and phrases year after year, and, like a worn-out gramophone record, he finally gives out, never having got within sight of the goal he talked so much about.

Comes the awakening to man, and if he be unafraid, he will find that the Christ within is not a teacher but a revelator of that which is and eternally has been; that instead of teaching of and about healing, prosperity, and happiness, he is revealing these true states of mind as inescapable—yea, as inescapable as the opposite states were formerly. He then stops the silly attempting to set things right in a universe that is run by law and order, and enters in upon the process of revelation. He reveals the inner things, the secret things that have been so from the beginning of the universe. He reveals, shows forth, that which is true and perfect. He is no more concerned about the letter, knowing that when the revelation is once recognized, the letter will take care of itself. He is not concerned about the outcome, knowing that a rubber ball thrown against a stone wall will return without any effort on his part. He knows that a word released from the center of his being is bound to accomplish whereunto it is sent, and, knowing this, he is not concerned or worried about the outcome.

Most of us have spent endless hours trying to make the return action something different from the sending action of the ball. But the ball can only return with the same force with which it was released. There is no chance for the word to go astray or to fail to find its own; all this is under the divine direction, which is above the frailty of human law and order. Human law changes constantly, but the divine law and order remaineth, and nothing is added to it and nothing is taken away.

Gradually confidence is established in the God-power which is constantly revealing itself to the one who is ready to lay aside human accoutrements and accept the glorious power of the Sons of God. Confidence to stand, having done all—having recognized the eternal rightness of the God-universe—he is unafraid to rest. He pushes the borders of his tent farther out into glorious new fields of untried expression and finds to his joyous surprise that new avenues are opening up to him. Undreamed of possibilities lie before him, for at last he has come to a place where he *believes* in the reality of the Kingdom as here and now and himself a revelator.

To the revelator comes the understanding of the unconditional Power—that indescribable thing which is seen to operate in a supernatural way yet which could never be anything but natural; that power which set aside the laws of the three-dimensional plane without regarding them as existent.

To a child playing a game, a chalk line may represent a prison, and as long as he abides under the rules of the game, he will act in accord with that and will accept it as a barrier to his freedom. When he is through with the game, however, he drops the whole thing and finds himself free and, of course, realizes at the same time that he was never anything else but free. His acceptance of that which constituted a prison was all that made one for him.

To the grown-up child, many prisons exist in just the same way. He accepts certain limitations of health, wealth, and happiness and is hypnotized to the belief, and eventually he finds himself helpless. If he suddenly comes to an understanding of himself as the Son of the living God and reveals to himself the freedom of the Son, then there happens in his life a miracle, or the working of some supernatural power. But in reality, it is merely the outpicturing of a natural state of the Son of the living God—recognized, revealed.

I am a revelator of the living Word—*I* am the revelator of the living Word—and *I* am therefore not surprised that the thing decreed shall come to pass. A stone thrown into the air will certainly come down without any aid from the one who threw it; so the word of the revelator will certainly return to him freighted with results, and he will not have to care about its return. That will automatically take place. "My own shall come unto me" by a sure and certain way. Why worry then?

Some will say, "What, am I to do nothing?" And if you have not gone further than to ask this question, I can only advise you to drop the book in the nearest wastebasket; it is not for you.

O glorious revelator within me, let thy light shine
out through the beliefs that have bound me!

When you arrive at the consciousness that you are ready to lay your Isaac on the altar, then you find that it is not necessary to give up anything in order to have heaven here and now. But the willingness to give up your Isaac without a question or doubt entering into the proposition can come only to the one who believes actually in God—believes that there is a God which expresses, regardless of whether he prays or not; believes in a God which could not do other than express eternally of His bountiful nature. Understanding God in this fashion will make it easy to let go of symbols in order to acquire the reality.

Many people believe—or at least they act as if they do—that God is perfectly static until they tell Him what to do, what to get rid of, and what to bring into manifestation, and for this reason they recite long man-made prayers, when the true prayer is "Be still ... be still." This is one of the last revelations to come to man, because he will not listen. He is so busy telling the world what is wrong with it and peddling the truth for a price that he has no time to be still. He feels within himself that if he were to be still the world would forget him, and so he has to keep shouting to the world how much he knows about the truth.

But surely the revelation of the Silence will eventually come into being, and man will find that by being still something will be told him which will, from then on, settle all questions regarding the right course to pursue. A revelation as deep as the infinite will be made unto the still soul—something will take place within which will burst the shell of human consciousness and free him into a new and finer growth-expression.

"This is my beloved Son, in whom I am well pleased" was addressed to a soul that could be silent. Have you ever been called that? Do you want to be? Then be still. Cease the chattering of and about, and be still, for when you hear those words pronounced over you, you can rest assured that your expression from that time on will be pleasing in the sight of God—and nothing else matters.

"Though ten thousand fall at thy right side, it shall not come nigh thee" only means that the still soul has heard and is able to understand the indestructible nature of Spirit. No man from the standpoint of reason can bring it about. That, and a lot of other things that man has failed to demonstrate, come with the revelation of the Silence. Be still; *I* have many things to say to you when you are ready to listen—when you are ready to be still.

When in the stillness *I* tell you the promises, then they are ready for fulfillment. When *I* say to you in the silence—or rather, when *I* impress you with such a thing as "My grace is sufficient for thee," you will from that time know that you are no more under the law of former human beliefs, but you are under grace, and this will be a new secret to you, a precious secret. It will be so wonderful that you would no sooner think of repeating it just to make conversation than a fearful banker would leave his vault open overnight. Silence will come to you and with it the gold, and with it the too, too precious truth that must not be cast to the swine of human thought. It will become so obvious that it will not be necessary for you to relate what it has done for you. Little trick demonstrations may please the child, but revelation is quite another thing.

I have many things to say to you when the burning, fiery coal has touched your lips and you are still. *I* have something to tell you about time and space that no man shall write on paper but which *I*; through the man Jesus, showed forth to those who had eyes. Instantly is not soon enough for Me to act, but it is the shortest measure the human mind can grasp. Be still; *I* have things to tell you. *I* will never leave you. *I* will speak to you through any and every channel. Fear not; *I* know your every need and will bring it into manifestation in the easiest possible manner when you are ready to see Me.

Go out, then, and consider the lily—you must be still when you consider a thing, but consider the lily—and if you have seen what *I* have had to show you there, you will not be running about like a ship without a rudder, asking first one and then the other what to do and how to do it and getting a different formula from each one, only to become a mass of complexities and confusion. Be still. *I* shall eventually be able to show you some of the mysteries.

Beloved, when you are still and you hear Me say, "My grace is sufficient for thee," then will you know the joy of the giver of good; then will you see the veil rent asunder, and you will stand before the throne of your own soul, nothing lacking, not asking favors but appropriating the gifts of the infinite Godhead which pour out upon you in such abundance. You shall be called by a new name, a new and secret name, and in a twinkling you shall be changed.

Do you hear? *I* am speaking to you as clearly as *I* can through the medium of the printed page. Fear not; *I* (the Consciousness once awakened) will never leave you, and *I* know all things. If any lack wisdom, let him ask of God and let him know that God is within himself, and that is the only point of contact he can possibly have with God. God within your own consciousness will supply you with every bit of information necessary if you ask and are ready to be still at the same time. If you contemplate Me, the I AM, as the God within, then you will know that the limitations of the human personality are broken. Be still. Let Me reveal Myself to you in a way which will cause you to know the Allness of the Kingdom here and now.

And as we have borne the image of the earthy, we shall also bear the image of the heavenly (1 Cor. 15:49).

This glorious change will take place when the new birth takes place, when man realizes that he is here and now a being of Spirit and is willing to walk in new ways. What has a butterfly to do with the ways of a caterpillar? What have you to do with that from which you have evolved? Why turn back and imagine that you still have to muck over the difficulties overcome or not overcome? Why rehearse things of the past which belong to the caterpillar life? You are a new creature, and as surely as you have borne the out-picturing of the consciousness of a creeping caterpillar, so you shall bear the image and capacities of the butterfly. As surely as you have borne the image of the long-suffering human personality, with its tremendous limitations, so you shall bear the image and have the capacities of the Son of God—of the living God. Dare you to take your good here and now?

How silently the change must take place. Hid away in the cocoon of secrecy, the ugly, limited caterpillar goes its way, with a whole avalanche of condemnation, hatred, limitation, and other difficulties. It is not announced to the world that he will transform himself, or else the curious, disbelieving world would tear his cloak of secrecy from him and kill him. So will it be with you when you are ready to go into your cocoon of silence. *I* can bring to you a greater change than that which happens to the caterpillar. When you are ready, *I* will do the work.

When you can be still and are ready to lose everything that has to do with the caterpillar, then *I* will make the transformation. But if you, in your heart, imagine that you shall be transformed for the sole purpose of rushing about calling attention to the fact that you were once a caterpillar and are now a butterfly and therefore great and wonderful, you may stay in your shell of secrecy from now on and nothing will happen. *I* am not concerned with the telling of truth but with the revelation of its boundless and priceless glories. Be still.

O beloved, presently you shall be lost in the immensity of this glorious power, and the trifling events of the human personality will be so much thistledown before the hurricane. To your opened eyes, you will see that such wondrous fields of attainment lie ahead that the village you are leaving must be wiped out of memory.

Be still. Let Me reveal Myself. Let Me tell you something. Let Me fill you with the Spirit of fire and water, and let Me send you forth into expression, a burning flame of revelation and a thirst-quenching fountain of life. You! You, the little insignificant thing that you are, or you, the great pride-swollen manifestation that knows so much and has so much or bears such a wonderful name and are covered with fame. You, you who read—throw off the mantle of this human self and lose yourself in Me. Then you will know of the limitless blessings and freedom of the Son of the living God. Do you hear, you who read this page? You?

Chapter XIII

Believest Thou This?

"Whom do men say that I am?" Some say one thing, some another; some may consider you a religious bigot, a holier-than-thou, a thief, a liar. It makes little difference what answer is made to that question, but the answer to another question determines your place in the grand scheme of heaven here and now—"But whom do *you* say that *I* am?"

Whom do you say that *I* am?—you, yourself—what do you say of your I AM? Do you say that it is a miserable worm of the dust that needs constantly to be treated, led, and helped? Or is it the creation of the living God? When will you answer, "I am the Son of the living God" and proceed to reveal this Man of God to the universe here and now?

In a moment you think not—when the seemingly cease-less thinking about how to make God do your bidding stops—at that point, the Christ comes into manifestation. Not much Christ-Consciousness or power can penetrate the layers of human thought, which form an insulation about you. Reasoning about God does not make Him any more visible than He is already. "No man shall see God and live" is paired oft with the statement "In my flesh shall I see God." In the realm of the human intellect, little or no wisdom is seen; a strange chain of coincidences hooks a train of cars together, each with its load of thought and care. There is to the human mind little actual reason for man being here. He has often asked himself "Wither?" and "Why?" These go unanswered, and he finds that man's days are full of trouble. A lovely picture for a God creation, to be sure!

Ah, but when he takes his attention away from appearances and can answer himself, "You are the Son of the living God," the whole fabric of hell breaks through and the heavenly light of Self-revelation shines out here and now into expression. Man finds himself clear-seeing, clear-hearing, clear-speaking, revealing the kingdom of heaven here and now, appropriating the good and passing it on to the universe. He finds new and lovelier capacities. He perceives himself to be the Son of the most High, with dominion and authority. He finds himself in affluence. He finds the glory of Self-expression here and now. A thousand avenues open before him. He finds it wonderful. The consciousness is deepened and made more receptive—made ready for the things *I* could not tell you back in Jerusalem because you could not have borne the glory of it all. The eyes are aware of a new and lovely universe here and now, peopled with angelic beings instead of fiends incarnate.

Who do you say that *I* am? What are the capacities? And no wonder it was given to the child! The child would automatically answer yes to "Believest thou this?"—but the adult, wise in his own conceit, tries to reason it out. He says he would like to, but his eyes are so hypnotized to evil that he cannot. That is why the Christ has said to take your attention away from appearances and rest it on the Isness of Being. "Judge not from appearances, but judge righteous judgment"—the judgment of the Son of God.

Can you believe it is possible for the perfect health you have sought so long to be manifested in you now? I did not ask whether you desired it or wanted it; I asked whether you can believe that it is possible. The subtle word contains the connecting link of manifestation; it is the way through which the unseen suddenly becomes seen. The visible-invisible appears.

"Believest thou this?" was asked over and over by Jesus, and when the answer was "Yea, yea, Lord," the results were sure to follow.

Just what do you believe? Many people know the letter of truth perfectly but are not healed. I may have at my command the whole technique of playwriting and be but a critic, with no ability whatsoever to write even a small scene. You may know a hundred systems of truth, but that does not make you a revelator of the kingdom—no, not until you believe it is possible.

Not until you get over the emotional worship of Jesus and "go thou and do likewise" can you ever know the beauty of the Kingdom here and now. When you sit down to have your quiet time of contemplation and are done with the insane idea of trying to make God do your bidding or of following some words rattled off by some other person—then you will ask yourself, "Believest thou this?" And when you can say, "Yea, Lord" within yourself, the manifestation is as good as into visibility. Believest thou this?

Chapter XIV

When Ye Pray

True prayer is not demanding things of the universe; nor yet is it imagining that things can be had by begging or beseeching or yet knowing they are yours. Prayer is merely recognition of that which is about to appear—provided, of course, you are willing to accept your good. "Thank you, Father" was one of the most efficacious prayers ever said, and it was followed up by a magnificent explanation of the nature of prayer: "I knew it was already so." This checks perfectly with the statement "Before they call, I will answer; and while they are yet speaking, I will hear."

When we get over the idea of praying to a man-god, we shall see that prayer is merely aligning ourselves with the power of that which is due to appear in our lives. In like manner, affirmations in their truest sense do not and cannot change the eternal nature of the universe; they are the words which are uttered because of the urge of the thing pressing upon the individual for expression. Hence, instead of any more of the prodigality comes the Sonship that, instead of begging for life, partakes of life as his inheritance and names his statement of this fact as an automatic result, just as one who is sitting in darkness will automatically exclaim, "Oh, light!" when a sudden shaft of light pierces the gloom. It is not said with an idea of creating light but as a full recognition of the existence of light at that place and time.

The person standing in front of a mirror does not exist because of the reflection in the mirror but vice versa. We have reversed the very processes of life and have been working at them blindly and backwards. No wonder our results have been so meager and unhealthy. When the prayer is uttered out of a full heart, with a full recognition, you who read this page will take your good in this manner; your heart will almost burst with the fullness of this truth—awareness of My presence and of all the things you have so long sought for.

> Come ye, buy, and eat ... drink ... without price (Isa. 55:1). Take no thought ... are ye not better than many ravens? (Luke 12:22, 24).

Do you not understand what you have been doing? When will you speak out of the full heart of recognition that there is such a thing as a God present here and now in all His fullness? The old order shall pass away. A new heaven and a new earth shall descend out of the clouds of your belief.

A new heaven is not a heaven patched up and made livable; it is a new heaven, and the new heir comes to take his place. He is all new and glistening, all glorious and free. "Former things have passed away." Do you hear? You who read this page? You?

When ye pray, the whole soul is at attention. It is so absorbing—this recognition of God within, without, everywhere—that man easily forgets his needs. He is swallowed up in the sea of All-substance and is content, and he becomes aware of his own. Be still, be joyously still. You are atop the heights of manifestation. Do you hear? You who read this page? You?

It is so absorbing, so radiantly absorbing, the glory of the God-Son and his kingdom, that nothing matters, and therefore everything matters. In the Absolute Reality, when you lose your life, you find it. When you lose the tiny, limited personal sense of life, you lose all the irritating beliefs that go with it—petty wants and its straining to be famous or great.

> Wist ye not that I must be about my Father's business? (Luke 2:49).

Where is the Father, and what is His business? Over and over, this is called to your attention, for a moment's consciousness of this fact will cause you to function in your right place—will cause great and mighty peace to surge over you. You cannot be out of place as long as this awareness is with you. Your Father's business is the business of Self-expression. When you are expressing the true Self, you are bringing in the kingdom of heaven, for you are, both literally and figuratively, giving water to the thirsty and food to the hungry; in other words, the urge of Spirit as a reality is gushing forth into conscious expression.

The Father's business is Self-revelation. You will reveal yourself to yourself, and no more will you sit in sackcloth and ashes, wishing for that which is already yours. Do you hear? You who read this page? You?

Let go; be quiet; it is well. All is well; heaven is here and now. *"Blessings, blessings, blessings—so many you cannot count them."* Did you hear? Cease from the argument. Seek peace and pursue it; thereby all good shall come unto you. All is enough. Why worry? I speak to you from out these pages and say to you," It is well." Do you hear? Then rest.

There shall be no sluggish waiting and imagining things; action is My name. *I do—I am.* Be at peace. When the moment comes, you shall be fully equipped to run the race of certain attainment. You shall be able to write so that he who runs may read and he who reads may run. Everything you give to another you increase a thousand-fold when it is given in love and not for gain.

> There is he that scattereth, yet tendeth to increase; and there is he that withholdeth ... but it tendeth to poverty (Prov. 11:24).

All the human ideas are reversed in the truth.

What went ye out for to see? (Matt. 11:8).

Do you go out to see a man with a reputation or run after a book that is said to contain the key? When you realize that the I AM within you is the key to every person, place, and thing, you will begin to unlock the treasures of your own kingdom. You will then be able to release the hidden springs of inspiration in a book or within your soul and see the new life fill everything.

Stop the condemnation of your beautiful Self. "If ye deny me (Christ within), I shall also deny you." In other words, if you find Me incapable of governing your life, then no matter how you call upon Me, I shall not answer because of your "unbelief," because you do not honestly believe it is possible for the inner Lord to rule absolutely and harmoniously in your life. If you have a house, consciousness, divided against itself, it will fall—and so you will fall and attempt to work out your problem by praying to a God afar off, a tyrant that may hear your prayers, a God of wrath and hatred.

Stop thinking of yourself as a worm of the dust; stop judging yourself; stop the everlasting talking about that which is past and dead. Arise, and let the dead bury their dead. Do not try to straighten out things. Get yourself lined out with the power within, and you will find things automatically falling into harmony and order. The piece of steel follows the magnet, but you are trying to make the magnet follow the piece of steel. God cannot be made to do your bidding, but by becoming conscious of your point in the universal Mind, you will be happy in doing His bidding. You will someday cheerfully say, "Not my will, but thine be done" and be satisfied that it is the only will and is the door of freedom, not martyrdom. Be still—nothing is hard to Me. Do you hear? You who read this page? You?

Dominion is yours through the recognition of the Christ within, dominion to do and to be. The Christ asks no favors to perform. He does not need the recommendation or veto of anyone. He is independent of such three-dimensional rubbish. The dawn asks no permission to dispel the night; it may not be in accord with many people's desires to have it come when it does, but it is above requesting the favor to express. So you will likewise ask no privilege to speak the freeing word of truth nor to perform the works after the manner of Jesus.

The wind bloweth where it listeth, and thou hearest the sound thereof, but canst not tell whence it cometh, and whither it goeth; so is everyone that is born of the Spirit (John 3:8).

So, then, is every man, for every man is born of the Spirit when he arises to recognize this. He comes and goes, and no one shall say him no, and no one shall know how he cometh or goeth, for the ways of Spirit are past finding out. "My ways are past finding out," but My ways are ways of definite accomplishment—effortless, untrammeled, and free; unconditioned and easy into expression, assembling instantly all that is necessary for the instantaneous expression of the Son of God.

Thus, when you are ready to let the Christ within take over the government of your life, you will find the upper chamber, the robe and the ring, the scrip and purse always waiting for you. Are you afraid? Dare you accept such a wondrous gift? Perhaps you plead that you are unworthy, and you are—unworthy because you are judging the Christ within by the standards of your limited human capacity. Having eyes, ye see not, and ears, ye hear not, and hence, you judge from the blinded and deaf state of human reasoning and find such a glorious attainment impossible.

"In the twinkling of an eye" is the manner of His coming in—"the moment ye think not." Who by thinking can find Me? "Who by taking thought can add one cubit unto his stature?" But at a moment when you think not—when you have done with the idea that you can force God to appear and do your bidding by merely thinking of Him, and have come to the recognition of the Presence which is past all limitations and conditions—you will say, "Whereas I was blind, now I see" and perceive a wholly new world about you.

Many are the seekers after truth who think that by affirmations they can call up God and order Him to set things right, just as Aladdin is supposed to have done with his lamp. They fail to have the symbology of the true Aladdin with his Lamp—*Light*—but imagine that if they say it often enough, it will work.

A new system is discovered; it is tried with great avidity and then found wanting. So shall it be: "I shall overturn and overturn, until he comes whose place it is to rule "—until *I* am the only ruler of your universe, and every prop is kicked from under and you stand revealed to yourself, a glorious Son of the living God with healing in his wing, with light in his eyes, with his feet shod with the winged sandals of attainment clothed in Light.

Praying without ceasing is the prayer of thanksgiving and recognition. When ye pray, say "Thank you, Father"— remembering where Jesus told you the Father resided— and rest. And having done all, stand and see the salvation, the coming into manifestation of the Power of God here and now. You who read this page, do you hear? You?

Chapter XV

Three Planes

The three planes of existence—Matter, Mind, Spirit—referred to as three measures of meal, which eventually all become leaven, explain themselves somewhat after this fashion:

Matter Plane. Here matter is used to heal matter. Medicine is poured into matter with the hopes of healing it. Man earns his living by the sweat of his brow. He belongs to the classification "you say it is four months until harvest." He says it takes time for man to grow; he is a creature of time and space and all the laws he concocts by looking at the appearances of things. Finally, having exploded one material remedy after another, he turns to the process of thought.

Mind Plane. Here man thinks, or attempts to think, his way out of difficulties. He believes that by thinking along a certain line he will arrive at the desired end. He goes so far as to believe that he can prosper himself by merely thinking he is prosperous. He believes he can heal disease by thinking there is no disease. When confronted by the millions of failures along the line, he says it is not merely thinking, but knowing, that will make the difference; but in spite of the fact that many things have been known for ages, no results have followed. It is a known thing that the Master walked on the water, but that does not mean the knower of this fact can do the same thing. He may know perfectly how to treat, and also that perfect health is man's heritage, and die while he is in the very process of "knowing the truth," as he calls it.

He may, and probably does, think and know that "all that the Father hath is mine," but it does not follow that he has enough to live on. From time to time his "work" seems to have been effective, but much of it has failed utterly. There is no set formula, no way of approaching the world of thought. One system tells him to enter from one end; another tells him diametrically the opposite.

We are taught concentration; we are taught relaxation; and we are taught to speak as one having authority. But until we obey the law which says "and I say unto you, take no thought for your life, what ye shall eat or what ye shall drink: nor yet for your body what ye shall put on" and "which of you by taking thought can add one cubit to his stature?" we will ever be fussing about, trying to think ourselves out of difficulties and finding in the last analysis that we have largely been under self-hypnosis.

If the law states clearly that nothing is to be changed by thinking, then why does man persist in trying to think himself out of difficulties? A survey of the thinking process of making success, happiness, and health shows clearly that there is more failure than success.

No matter what your opinion may be regarding the subject, you never will change anything in reality by your thought process. If the eternal verities were to be changed by the mere thinking of man, the whole of existence would be at the mercy of man, and chaos would result. The only thing that is changed by thinking is your attitude toward a thing.

Some people think that meat is harmful to them, others that they cannot do without it. What about this? Is the help or harm in the meat? "As a man thinketh in his heart, so is he" is a clear summing up of the man from the mental plane. It does not follow that because you think a certain way that makes it the same for another. Because you think a thing is good does not necessarily make it so. At one time it was thought to be good to force religion on people, obliging them to attend religious services. Today this is changed.

Only beliefs can be changed—realities never can. And so man again finds that he is up against a shifting, changing system of thought. He has beseeched, begged, pleaded, and even demanded what he claimed was his divine heritage, without the slightest results. He has lived upon some far distant demonstration of the Power and has drained it of its inspiration, hoping against hope that he might have a return of the Power. He has asked himself and others why it is that he is unable to heal or get healed, and eventually he turns to the plane of Spirit.

Spirit. "*I* am of too pure eyes to behold iniquity" is the watchword. Man begins to understand that the Power of the Christ-consciousness, which is quicker than the thought, is awareness and not creation. For the first time, he sees that his eye has been double, that he has been living in a world of good and evil; that he has had to accept evil before he could get rid of it; that if he could get rid of it, it of necessity must have been unreal. He sees that belief is the only thing that can be changed and that the eternal laws of God cannot be broken. If they could, they would be worthless. What man does is to attempt to break them and is himself broken in the attempt.

Awareness of his God-Self lifts him to a place of recognition. He sees clearly that all evil is ignorance (ignoring God). Just as a student of music who ignores the principles of harmony will achieve small results and much discord, so his acceptance of evil as something that has to be got rid of is merely his ignorance of the Something that must be recognized. In spite of the injunction "take no thought," thousands of people are today fighting a terrific battle with evil, which is more or less real to them by reason of their acceptance of it.

"Come out from among them (your beliefs) and be ye separate." You can believe anything, but that does not make it true. Eventually man will take the path of pure Christ-Truth, as manifested by Jesus, and will learn, as

Father Divine has often stated, "There is no BC. There is only BJ." There is no time which is before the Christ-consciousness. "Before Abraham was, I am," but there is a very definite period prior to the Jesus. The Jesus comes and goes, but the Christ remains in His changeless state of glory, waiting always for recognition. If Jesus had not recognized his true Self, the Christ, he would have passed away unknown, a little, obscure carpenter in a small village. He admitted that as Jesus he could do nothing, but that with the Christ he could do anything. He made it perfectly clear that what he did through the man Jesus is a present possibility with every man, knowing the impersonal Power which was and is impartial and everywhere instantly available.

Man begins to see that he cannot change the eternal facts of Being. Thousands have said, "Lord, Lord," and received nothing. Thousands have said, "Peace, peace," and there was no peace. And thousands have said, "Peace, be still," and seen a raging sea of human belief calmed like a millpond at sundown. No authority rests in the plane of the mental, for its basis is constantly changing.

Not so long ago, people believed that every true prayer should be prefaced with endless denials. This being eventually found unproductive of results, the idea was changed to intense and repeated affirmations of the truth. This too is beginning to crumble. Trying to take the kingdom of heaven by violence has not proved successful. Telling the Creator that he is God, and the only Creator, is no revelation to God and does not make it any more true than repeating a thousand times over that two times two is four makes it more four than it was before. It has always been that and always will; nothing will ever change that, for it is an eternal verity.

Gradually man begins to see that all his thought pro-cesses have come to naught; he has merely built up a universe of beliefs which he finds tumbling down about him. In his desperation, he reaches out for the reality of the spiritual plane, the place of changeless reality, and begins to experience the first real and enduring peace he has ever known—the peace which passeth all understanding. He sees now that the injunction "I will overturn and overturn, until he comes whose place it is to rule" is made true, and he is happy at last to be rid of the bulky letter of that teaching which was given to the child and kept from the prudent.

Why man has gone so far afield is the amazing thing, when he begins to see the simplicity of life and the beauty and holiness of the true creation. He smiles when he thinks with Shakespeare "there is nothing either good or bad, but thinking makes it so," and he sees the utter impossibility of such a creation proceeding from God. Imagine a world that is constantly subject to change by taking thought!

Awakening to the glorious possibilities of the Sons of God, man is Self-revealed. In a burst of glory, he suddenly sees the portals of heaven (self-expression) loom white and glistening before him. He begins to experience here and now his heaven. He calls from the watchtowers of the universe: "It is wonderful! It is wonderful! It is wonderful!"

His Name, the name of your I AM, is wonderful, and the government of the life of your Jesus, your human personality, shall be upon his shoulders.

Beloved, rejoice; it is wonderful. All the tiresome job of governing this erratic personality, which you have called by a special name, falls away. You take My yoke upon you and find My burden is light. My burden is merely the bearing of the testimony to the world that the law of a changeless Universe is here and now effective, and that the Sons and Daughters of God are not in any way subject to the limitations of the human personality. Man begins to see that true prayer means alignment with that which *is*. All "thine and mine" passes away, and the divine Ours comes into being.

It is wonderful! It is wonderful! It is wonderful! "Heaven and earth are full of thee." Think of it! You are living, moving, and having your being in the pure substance of Spirit. You do not have to think it into manifestation; you have to recognize that Jesus was a truthsayer and not a liar when he said, "The kingdom of heaven is at hand—it is within you." Believest thou this?—you who read this book—or will you drag in your dead fathers and your qualifications and your limitations and your special brands of teaching?

When the eye becomes single, the whole body is full of light—full, not nearly full. Full to overflowing because it has lost the shadow of belief which says there is evil in the universe and that thinking can change it into good. When the eye is single, it will perceive reality instead of belief and will thereby see reality into manifestation everywhere. It is wonderful.

Before you, who read this book, a new door has opened, the door of Christ. "I am the door," and at the same time, "Behold, I stand at the door." When you, through the process of recognition, know that there is such a thing as a perfect universe, created and sustained by God, who found it very good, you will, by opening the door of your human consciousness, find that *I* am there, ready to enter into expression. The I AM is your individual expression of the universal God. And no sooner is the door opened than you find that the I AM (your own individual point in consciousness) is the door of every wall, to every room (new state of consciousness), to everything that formed a shell about your good and which you termed problem. Behold! Behold! It is *I*, your real Self. Be not afraid. It is wonderful. It is wonderful. It is wonderful.

Quicker than thought is the thinker of the thought; quicker than any human measure is the I AM —knowing everything, needing nothing, awaiting recognition. *I* must increase—the Christ-consciousness must come more and more into visibility—and you (human beliefs) must decrease. The going of the personality, with its petty desire for fame or name or its holier-than-thou, stone-casting propensities, must decrease in order that the Son of God may come to rule in His own universe.

Contemplation of the perfect universe—not the attempt to create it—will cause your human universe to take on new proportions. The borders of your tent will be enlarged; you will launch out into deep waters: you will sing a new song, and that song will be "It is wonderful." To be absent from the body and present with the Lord is not an emotional experience but a present possibility. To be present with your true Self is to find yourself in possession of everything that is necessary to sustain the no-problem state of existence. It is wonderful!

Chapter XVI

The No-Treatment Man

The answer already exists to any and every mathematical equation you can or ever will think of. No matter whether you know it or not, it equals a certain thing before you even put it down on paper. Because you do not know it does not mean anything. Because you do know it does not make it so. It is already so. A problem exists only so long as the answer is unknown; the moment you have the answer, you have no problem. A question does not exist after you have the answer. It is merely converted into a statement of fact—a worked-out problem is no problem. This checks perfectly with the statement of the Master, "Before you ask I will answer, and while you are yet speaking I will give it unto you." The answer to every human problem (belief) exists before you express the belief.

We see the type-man Jesus overshadowed and finally swallowed up by the Christ-Self. Christ never had a problem; he never had to be healed, helped, prospered, or set in his right place. Jesus experienced all of these things. You could not heal Christ, but Jesus might be helped or treated. We see the escape from the misery of the Jesus-man made by recognition of the Christ. The moment he functioned in the Christ-consciousness, anything and all things were possible to him, but when he dropped down to the human plane of the Jesus, he cried, "My God, why hast thou forsaken me?"

Jesus came under the law of birth, breeding, training, environment, and all the rest. He had a history of his own and a human destiny, even as you have, which was blotted out, made nil, by the understanding of his true Self, which was above help. We see the Jesus in the process of recognizing his true Self and escaping the limitations of the human. In the press of the crowd, there was little escape for Jesus. But the Christ was able to take Its manifestation through the crowd unnoticed because the Christ in each has a way "that ye know not of"—and that is not the way of thought, for "eye hath not seen, nor ear heard, neither have entered into the heart of man, the things which God hath prepared for them that love him."

The Jesus, or what you might term his human personality, could see no way—he could not think his way out or across the lake unless he went through the limitations of the Jesus-consciousness. But turning to the true Self and recognizing Its presence enabled him to work what people called a miracle, which in reality was but the natural and true expression of the God-Self. It is no miracle for the hungry to be fed in the All-substance of God.

When Jesus said, "Wist ye not that I must be about my Father's business?" he had already made it clear that his Father was within. He might have stated clearly, "Wist ye not that this Jesus must be about the business of the I AM in me?" In other words, it should be about the business of that Power which does not bow down to the laws of the human limitation. This comes by a process of pure recognition, awareness.

Either the Scriptures are true, or they are a lie. What will you do with such statements as "You say there are yet four months, and then cometh the harvest, but I say unto you, lift up your eyes and look on the fields; for they are white already to harvest ... thrust in the sickle"?

Jesus could not reap where he had not sown any more than you can, but the Christ could thrust in the sickle because He did not in any way function under the frail laws of the human consciousness; hence, the importance of recognizing the Father within—not pleading with It, but merging the human will and thought unto It and acting from the point of awareness. If God cannot do it, neither you nor ten thousand people are going to accomplish it.

It is no longer a question of demonstrating good. It is a question of getting people to recognize that there is such a thing as God. Most anyone will challenge that statement, but a short conversation with most truth students will clearly prove that they believe more in the power of evil than good. Fifteen minutes of conversation will reveal evil of every sort as being stronger and more powerful than good. Few there be who salute the Christ in you and speak the word of Reality. They believe emphatically that evil has to be destroyed, and yet we find that there is nothing in the kingdom of God that can be destroyed. We find that in the Book of Life "nothing can be added to or taken from" the Word, remembering that the Word was made flesh.

What, then, is all this adding of evil and disease that has taken place? It is failure to recognize that there is such a thing as God. How could there be God and something else, if God is All in all? What is the evil that we treat but belief in a power opposed to the supreme Power. A human law is only local. Sin might be said to be somewhat a matter of geography. In order to fulfill a traffic law in one country, you may be deliberately breaking a traffic law in another.

"Ignorance of the law excuses no man" is more true on the divine plane of the no-treatment-man than on the human plane. In fact, you have paid every penalty of unhappiness and limitation by reason of the fact that you were ignoring the law of Spirit, which is "of too pure eyes to behold iniquity." On the human plane, you may run your car fifty miles an hour in a ten-mile zone and pay no penalty except you are apprehended, but this is not so in the universe of the All-God.

Were you to make a questionnaire for yourself and have to answer the question "Who are you?" what would you answer? Being perfectly honest, you would probably say, "My name is John Smith, thirty. I was born in California. I have thus and so much education, breeding, and family. I am subject to certain financial and physical limitations." But you have denied everything that is true. You are the Son of the living God. Do you hear? I said *living* God, not a God who has to be made alive by your thinking process or because you treat Him into existence or because you affirm that it is so. You are the Son—the point of manifestation where the God-Power pours out into expression in a constant and endless stream of power, health, substance, and holiness.

As you contemplate this glorious revelation, you will understand some of the wonderful possibilities that lie just ahead of your John Smith, through the door of the I AM consciousness, which is not created or made to appear by thought but which is recognized as the pure creation of God. Believest thou this? Do you actually believe that God made the world? If so, what are you going to do about it? If you make your bed in hell. there am *I*; if you ever recognize Me (Father within) in the most hellish situation you can imagine, you will see it instantly fade from the pictures and resolve itself into heaven. In other words, you will rend the veil of human belief and find the thing that you have been seeking standing eternally in its right place, merely waiting the coming of the Master, who would recognize it as true and stop trying to create it.

Is there actually any truth to the statement that God created the world, found it good, and rested, and that He is a changeless Power? Do you believe it? Or would you just like to believe it? Is it so that the kingdom of heaven is at hand? Or is that just a fairytale? Is it possible to have a host of sick, sinning, and evil things in heaven, in order that you may be glorified in treating them out of existence?

"Pray without ceasing" does not mean an endless, monotonous telling God about your troubles and of His qualities, but it does mean a constant capacity to be aware of the only living God as here and now and rejoicing over the presence of the Kingdom here and now.

No wonder such a magnificent thing is given to the child (the consciousness that can accept God without question) instead of the adult (adulterer), who mixes everything true with his impure reasoning. It has been said, "The wisdom of man is foolishness in the eyes of God and inversely, "The wisdom of God is foolishness in the eyes of man." Time without number, we find the wisdom of man failing ignominiously—what he learns one year as the height of erudition may the next year be relegated to the dump-heap of ignorance.

Three thousand years of medicine have not decreased disease, no matter how lofty the aims of those noble souls who have given of their best and even their human lives to make this end attainable. We are beginning to see that what Jesus and the prophets said is more than just a fairy tale. We begin to recognize that he spoke of a truth, for he spoke of himself. He spoke of the pure wisdom that was revealed by recognition that he was and *is* the Son of the living God. And just so soon as you begin to contemplate that state of things, you will see that what you have been trying to demonstrate for years is actually awaiting your appropriation.

The more we think of evil the more aggravated it becomes, until it increases to a point of self-destruction. Everybody has at one time or another built himself a Goliath and had it threaten his city (state of consciousness) with complete destruction, and at such time, he has called for his David with his five spiritual senses and destroyed or wiped out the manifestation of belief.

Eventually you will find that you have eyes and see, instead of eyes and see not. In other words, you will perceive what it means to become aware of your true Self. A body that is always in mind is a sick or ailing body; a pocketbook that is always in mind is flat; a state of life that is constantly toyed with in an attempt to make it better will only result in a poor manifestation. Rather, then, "be absent from the body and present with the Lord" sums up the teaching of recognition. When your thinking process is off of evil, evil ceases to function, for it is only sustained by the thought process. It has no divine mandate for existence and finds its substance in the ignorance of man, who thinks it is something real that he must call upon God to destroy. Just so long as he does this, he will operate on the mental plane of life and not experience the glorious freedom of the Child of the most High.

Job's captivity was changed when he stopped trying to change it. When he prayed for his neighbors, his captivity was turned, and he had twice as much as he had before. It is interesting that this should have happened after his almost ceaseless praying, beseeching, begging God to help him. We see very clearly that it is by taking thought that we produce the evil of life. The John Smith who does not recognize his true Self suffers with Job—he is always trying to save the world or himself instead of standing on the heights of Reality and revealing the kingdom of heaven as here and now. The Son of God is not a worker of miracles; he is a revealer of the finished kingdom. You are the Son of God—do you hear? And you are to reveal the kingdom of heaven as here and now. You begin to recognize why it is wonderful.

The no-treatment man is the Son of the living God. He lives constantly in heaven (a state of consciousness), and he speaks of himself. John Smith then takes up the word and goes through the mechanics and says, "I speak not of myself, but him that sent me into expression." We are at this very point of walking through the *door* and finding that, like a drop of water, we are one with the sea of substance, the sea of Spirit. As the candle flame is lost in the sunlight yet retains its individuality, so the individual loses his sense of separation and limitation and takes on the proportions of his God-given Self. He sees with the eyes of Spirit, which cannot behold evil. Not that he wants to shut his eyes to anything, but he actually sees as Jesus the Christ saw when he looked through the belief of ignorance that was binding a cripple and said, addressing the Christ in him, "Rise up and walk." The human personality had already testified to the fact that he could not move.

Jesus did not go to Lazarus to make him alive; he went to awaken him, stating that he had fallen asleep. Do you suppose the restoration of the withered arm was as slow as thought? It came instantly—the physical could not perceive its possibility because it saw with a glass, darkly, and saw the human history and reason as real. Jesus, through his at-one-ment with the Father within, perceived the man whole and perfect, and it was to this true Self that he addressed his command: "Stretch forth thine hand."

"He who hears, obeys," and when you come to understand your true Self, you will appropriate the gifts in a natural, normal way. Just as soon as the selfish seeking has gone and you realize the uselessness of self-seeking, you will be the avenue through which pours the endless stream of God-manifestation. To decree is to see it come forth. The Son of God, the no-treatment man who needs only to be recognized, approximates his spiritual qualities. He has the seeing eye, the hearing ear, and the gift of Self-revelation. Awake thou, Lazarus, bound up in the filthy grave clothes of thine own making; arise and shine, for thy light has come.

Now is the accepted time—now are we the Sons of God. Do you hear? A thousand petty despots who have the world to save will pass away, but My word shall not pass away. You are My word made flesh. You, John Smith, are the word of the I AM made flesh, and now we see the possibility of bringing up this garment to a higher and finer state of beauty and power. We begin to see that as we become better acquainted with the God-Self, the human garment will take on finer states of health, wealth, and happiness. These will follow naturally. Your contemplation will then be about "whatsoever things are pure, whatsoever things are lovely, whatsoever things are of good report," and you will see these words made flesh, dwelling among you.

Who are you, and to what end were you born? Are you just another bit of humanity, to be tossed about from one fearful experience to another—to go down into the grave of defeat? Or are you the Son of the living God *here* and *now* present, in full possession of your true capacity? Awake, awake, awake. It is wonderful!

Chapter XVII

Trailing Clouds of Glory

Our birth is but a sleep and a forgetting;
The soul that rises with us, our life's star,
Hath had elsewhere its setting
And cometh from afar;
Not in entire forgetfulness,
And not in utter nakedness,
But trailing clouds of glory do we come
From God, who is our home:
Heaven lies about us in our infancy!

—Wordsworth

Trailing clouds of glory, sweeping the great horizon of your new heaven and earth, follow after you, Son of the living God, in great swirls of light and illumination. No more can you withhold this wondrous light than day can stay its coming. No more the conscious effort to know the truth, to make others see the truth; no more straining to have people listen to your chatter about what is or is not—no more anything, but simply *Being*.

Why do you *try* to be? A thousand eager souls have gone down in defeat trying through every possible means to be that which they already were. "They have taken my Lord away" is the cry of a personality worshipper, one who looks to mankind for his salvation instead of looking to the only possible source of such power—that within his own consciousness.

Trailing Clouds of Glory follow after you, and the great illumination of their brightness goes before you. Are you afraid to accept such a glorious picture of your true Self? Then you are yet playing with the colored pebbles in the shallow waters of metaphysics, disobeying the command "launch out into deep waters." He who has the courage to "launch out" into the freedom of his soul, not asking of those beachcombers who hang around the shores of personal ideas, will find nothing wanting. The rough sea will be smooth, and the calmness shall be there—that deep stillness of being alone and for the first time being actually free from the soul hunger and loneliness that nothing of the human mind can satisfy.

Many who read these lines—perhaps you who are reading now—will be Self-revealed and will find it natural for the Son of the living God to have glorious trailing clouds of attainment follow after him—no matter whither he may go. The signs shall follow, they shall not precede. Why look ye for a signpost, when *I* am the way? Salute no man that thou passest along life's highway, for he may turn you awry. Salute the Soul of your true Self and be not turned aside. "It is I "—eternally *I*—and when you begin to see Me in everything, you will call Me out into expression, and that which flies at you in mad fury, trying to destroy you, shall be in an instant transformed into Me.

This whole process lies within the scope of you who read this page. I have said to you, "Agree with thine adversary quickly," and the agreement is made through calling the name of the living God out of the dead Lazarus. It is wonderful —everything is wonderful. The only thing that is dispelled at such a moment is your belief in evil. Even hell is made into heaven when you call upon Me. Call upon Me and *I* will answer. Do you hear? *I* said, "*I* will answer."

Believest thou this? Or are you going to argue a little and try to prove that it is so with a reservation? Go thy way; the bridegroom passeth, and you have no oil because you have not learned yet to accept your good. You are still with those who want to make it happen and who are looking for personal aggrandizement.

But one day—perhaps today, perhaps right now—you will shed the filthy rags of argument and of personal teaching, rise and go up into a high place and descend again, not to work out problems, but to reveal the God within you. As much as ye will, that give *I* unto you. Do you hear?

"Acquaint now (right while you are reading is now) thyself with him, and be at peace: thereby good shall come unto thee." How very simple—too simple, perhaps, because you have been hypnotized into believing that long, hard study was necessary to attain the kingdom and that you were full of sin that some sin cleanser had to take out of you by special instruction that he could give you. Yet shall *I* call again and again to you: "Acquaint now thyself with him, and be at peace: thereby good shall come unto thee." Do you see how utterly impossible it would be for you to explain the glorious feeling of "It is well" to anyone who was trying to think it out?

You are impressed with that which descends to the plane of human thinking from the place of Christ-consciousness, the fourth-dimensional realm. Do you not see what is meant by "Acquaint now *thyself* with him and be (find yourself) at peace: thereby all (the whole) good shall come unto thee"? Can you understand, then, that your expression of healing of whatever belief comes before you is merely the light of the Trailing Clouds of Glory which automatically emanate from your being? When you see this, that All (the whole) Good shall come unto you, then will you know that you have the hidden well of living water and the exhaustless substance of the manna that cometh down from heaven.

Do you see that you will be self-sufficient and that your giving will in reality be only the coming of your presence? On whomsoever your consciousness rests pours the infinite blessing and possibility of a perfect revelation of health, prosperity, or happiness. Should they but accept it, either consciously or unconsciously, the transformation will take place and they will shout, "Whereas I was blind, *now* (right *now* the *only*) I see"—and one blindness after another shall be healed in every man. New fields of illumination and light shall be made visible to him, and each time he shall exclaim, "Whereas I was blind, now I see."

Do you see that the mere acceptance of this makes it possible for you? Until you believe it is possible (not from a standpoint of credulity or blindly), it can never be possible to you, however much of the letter you may know. You believe in the true fashion of the Word when you have accepted the finished Kingdom as here and now and possible of expression. Then what matter if a thousand say to you, "It is hard ... there is much work and difficulty in attainment." *I* said to you many times—and *I* am saying to you (you who read this page, do you hear?) at this instant—that the kingdom of heaven is given to the Child, not in years but with the capacity that can accept good as real instead of endeavoring eternally to make My kingdom over or set things right by first believing in evil.

As soon as you take away the personal nature of evil, you have it in a place of understanding, where it can more easily be seen as nothing but belief. The thing you have been working on is your personal devil, and he is fed by the substance of your thought. Taking your attention away from the body—being absent from the body, or embodiment, of your problem and present with the Lord—is another way of putting it. When you are present with the Lord, the Trailing Clouds of Glory sweep the horizon of your universe and find nothing there which needs to be destroyed or killed, but find the great, glorious realm of attainment opening wide its portals to you. Enter.

"Where there is no vision, the people perish." Where there is no vision which is beyond the thought process, the people finally fall by the way, full of dead letter and earnest effort. The glorious vision of the Son of the living

God is yours. You are dream-drenched with the joy of it all; they pass before your gaze as lovely realities instead of phantoms and ghosts of dead hopes and wishes. Deeper and deeper you go into the great clouds of light; more wondrous are the revelations made to you as you go your eternal way of aloneness and attainment. Nothing shall be denied you—and no one shall say ye nay.

Do you hear? Can you talk this glorious thing over with one who has but a mind full of thoughts or trite statements and a house full of evil that needs attention? You shall learn the glory of silence which is golden by its light of revelation. Stand still … very still … stiller than any human mind can imagine.

Everything you touch shall be filled with the Spirit of Light. Everything you look upon shall be illumined with the glory. And all this not in the impractical way most people look upon these wondrous words, but in a way of concreteness. "Even in my flesh shall I see God." Do you begin to see that the impractical teaching is that which shows you how to get things when there is the great "Seek ye first the kingdom of heaven (within), and all things shall be added unto you"? Do you go any further until you have decided within yourself whether this is a lie or the truth—why continue the self-hypnotism any further? You are on the path of attainment, attainment of greater things than can possibly be set down in black and white.

Trailing Clouds of Glory shall follow you as you go about your Father's business, and the pygmy personality will fade out of the pictures as the new creature moves into the plane of expression From out the invisible will come new ideas and impressions that will cause you to know that the way of attainment is not fraught with difficulties, but is easy and beautiful, a way possible for the childlike consciousness which believes in its good and accepts it.

Out of the invisible comes the manifest. As a smile out-pictures a state of consciousness and is instantly reflected by all who come in contact, thereby making the increase infinite, so the idea which wells from the inner Lord will come into ample expression and be reflected back to the giver in endless ways. The whole concern is not how to make it reflect back with increase, but to release it without thought of return. A smile is given, not to get a smile in return, but because it is an automatic expression of the state of consciousness at that time. A grin will not accomplish the same results. Few are fooled. Few are those who respond. The deep, smiling consciousness of good shall be reflected back again and again in countless ways.

"Ye are the light of the world." What world? And who is referred to as *ye*? All these glorious promises and statements of absolute facts must at length be overtaken by the Son of the living God; he must finally come to cause everyone to yield its full measure of substance. It is only when the grape has been pressed in the winepress that the hull is thrown away, and it is when the inspiration has been taken from the letter that it falls by the way.

When will you rise and leave the tatters of human reasoning and former attainment for the open road of the Son of the living God? Dare you—you who read this page?—remembering that taking the open road does not of necessity mean a physical voyage. He who recognizes any of the attributes of the Christ-consciousness as so and real will see them into instant manifestation, as Peter, realizing the substance of freedom, could sing in a material prison and cause it to open to him. *I* am the way—if it takes an earthquake to do it, what of it? And those that put you in will invite you to come out so they may be blinded by the Trailing Clouds of Glory that follow after you.

Finally you will realize that the everlasting rising to heights and falling to depths is a matter of human belief and that it has nothing to do with the real, the lasting, the eternal, but is merely an emotional reaction. The Son of the living God does not ascend to heights and get cast off into the depths, for there is no height, depth, breadth, or length in the All—yet there are all of these as long as they are necessary for Jesus to operate within their boundaries. There is the glory of the risen Lord gleaming through you; the fashion of your countenance shall be changed, and you shall be revealed in a glory of light. Do you hear? Do you see? Do you look between the lines and grasp the hidden meaning that is there?

Go into all the world, preach the good spell. Speak of the good spell, the wonder of goodness that is everywhere, and go not out again, first to point out the evil and then hunt in your mental satchel for a remedy—one thing for headache, one for a mortgaged house, another thing for an inharmonious home, another for how to find money and a job. How long will you cast lots for a part of My garment? When will you see that to know Me is life eternal? Life eternal is not subject to disease and limitation; neither can it be made unhappy by the lack of anything. Can you see now, you who read this page, that a thousand years being as a day and a day as a thousand years, you can make the hypnotism of yesterday a thousand years old and out of your way.

You shall do all these things, and the mists of earth, the beliefs of the human limitations, shall vanish away in a cloud of light and beauty. Suddenly you shall walk untrammeled and free; a new door shall open unto you, and you shall enter. As you do, so it will close, and the past, with its limitations and fears, will be vanished away. Do you hear? You who read this page? You?

I speak to you. The new order of things is at hand, and it is the time of its appearance. It will be very much as the wakening from a dream that you fully intend to remember but about which is spun such a mist of forgetfulness that only the merest fragments remain. This is the translation from one mansion to another in the universal consciousness. Newer and fresher capacities shall be yours; you will find yourself in possession of wisdom necessary to perform that which you formerly thought impossible of attainment, and strange as it may seem for the moment, you shall presently find that it is quite natural. The moment you overtake a truth or become conscious of it, at that instant you also realize that you have always known that truth and that there has never been a time in your life when you did not have it actively into expression.

When you go by the Way, be sure you leave the false modesty of the hypocrite behind. Be not afraid to assume and take for granted the power of the Son of the living God. You are acting within your own precincts when you realize that the power of the Christ to accomplish that which it will is a natural thing and not something for display.

It is wonderful—and even as you have been reading this word, your fear and problem have melted away, dissolved by the Light shed from the Trailing Clouds of Glory that emanate from the Son of the living God. It is all right with you now; everything is all right—now. The fig tree that cumbered the ground has shriveled up and disappeared; the fig tree that did not obey the law to bring out the whole manifestation at the instant is also pulled up by the roots. The slow process of birth, growth, maturity, and fruition is all swallowed up in instant recognition of the perfect whole—the flower before the seed. He that hath ears, let him hear. Do you hear? The whole in perfect manifestation, not through the slow human process of time and space.

Feeding among the lilies, considering the lilies, the effortless, unlabored action of the I AM moving into a constant stream of expression. Rest, beloved; it is well with you. You are the glorious Being of Light in a Universe of Light. You are lost in the immensity of it all. As the candlelight is lost in the sunlight yet retains its individuality, so you are lost in Me, in the Spirit of the All, and there you find nothing wanting or lacking There you find no shadows. There your soul is singing the song of the Son of the living God in the eternal Now and Here, in the eternal joy of Life, Life, Life—complete and filled with an unspeakable joy. It is so. Do you hear?

Remember, then, as you go out into your kingdom of heaven about your Father's business, that the Trailing Clouds of Glory are about you and that it is well.

Chapter XVIII

The Blaze of Life

The Lord in the midst of thee
is strong and mighty.

The Lord, the Power, the Life, in the midst of the burning bush which blazes forth and yet which consumes not—which at the same time consumes that which is not—is strong and mighty. The Blaze of Life which you have theretofore thought of as a destroying flame proves to be a dazzling white light which shows the nothingness of that which it formerly seemed to consume.

There is nothing in the kingdom of heaven that needs to be destroyed. A seed that has expanded through the time and space belief of the human thinking has not been destroyed but fulfilled. The grub that through the slow motion of time and space thinking becomes a butterfly is not destroyed but fulfilled. So you will find that you have not great areas of evil in your mind and life to be destroyed but vast amounts of unrealized joy, happiness, and expression to be set free.

As long as the eye is double, you are a believer in hell, a purifying fire which is to consume something which you promptly say is nothing. What kind of mental gymnastics is this? You may say that you can prove it has to be destroyed—you can cite Scripture to that end—but, having the double eye of good and evil, you have never yet read the real Scriptures.

The Blaze of Life within you, if misinterpreted, may cause you to commit that which is designated evil. A bank robber's original idea is good. He desires to inherit the substance of mind, expressed in the symbols of the workaday world. But his interpretation is bad. Immediately upon receipt of the desire to possess substance, he translates it into terms of his limited universe. He finds it impossible to attain in any of the legitimate avenues, and so he proceeds to break human law in order to obtain it. His wanting the substance was not wrong; where he fell down was in looking to the appearances and, finding them limiting and impossible and accepting them as real, attempted to set them aside.

The first tendency of man after he has felt the urge of the oncoming good in his life is to look out in the world of illusion and see the limitations that are about him. He immediately judges—decides whether it is possible or not, whether it is reasonable or not. If he finds it reasonable with the human understanding, he proceeds to bring it into manifestation by human channels, but if not, he may turn criminal and attempt to produce it that way.

No wonder, then, that the Master said, "Judge not after appearances, but judge righteous judgment." If you are looking to the appearances of the human life, almost anything is impossible because it is subject to chance, destiny, fate, or what you will. When man learns that the life within the temple, body (embodiment), is a Blaze of Life, he will be able to see with this Blaze past the human barriers, of whatever nature they may be, and perceive the object of his desire in full manifestation.

Judging righteous judgment is accepting the words of the inner Lord: "Before ye ask *I* will answer, and while ye are yet speaking *I* shall give it unto you." Is this so, or is it a lie? Answer—you who read this page. Are you still playing with words? Do you still reel off metaphysical statements and find your coffers empty and your life cold and unexpressed? *I* am the Blaze of Life. Can you see how the light of this Blaze can search the joints and marrow, and how the stupid repeating of words will fall like shadows on snow? Can you see what "Be still and know" will do for you, instead of rushing about to find a healer or teacher or copying a statement out of a book or a lecture to repeat a thousand times?

Can you see what the Blaze of Life will do for you? It is sharper than a two-edged sword. It catches you eventually, as you ride along on the way to Damascus, all proud of your attainment—you, the official stone caster; you, the consecrated one. Is one more consecrated than another? Are not all of the same substance of life? Is not the Blaze of Life in every man who will turn within and find it?

So wonderful! That magnificent, incandescent purity radiating from the very essence of your being; that sacred halo proceeding from the very essence of the flowering fount of Life, is the message that, written on the fleshly tablets of your heart, is the fulfillment of the promise going before you, blessing, healing, and saving; giving life to the dead, delivering those who long have striven for perfection, release from bondage.

—Father Divine

So wonderful, that Blaze of Life within you which is the perfect expression of your true Self. Without Life and Light there is no expression; other than this, it is but a borrowed light, a flicker on the mirror of the human mind. The Blaze of Life within you is that white dazzling Light which illumines all you say; the most commonplace words become alive and full of fire, the most ordinary events become great waymarkers on the path of the new pilgrim. You, even though you be a simple carpenter or tender of sheep, will, with this light, find the gates of the king's palace flung wide open to you. You, though you be a fine nobleman, shall find the Blaze of Life dispelling the hateful bondage of a *poseur*. Your fatigue of always keeping up a pretense shall cease, and you shall find quiet and peace; pearls and rubies shall drop from your lips rather than the hard, worthless gold which formerly bought you nothing but the fawning of monkeys.

You, with the picture of your Self-expression hidden away in the shadows of limitation, shall suddenly find it illumed by the Blaze of Life—it will become alive and active, and strange as it may seem, you will find that all the waiting you have done will have amounted to nothing— you shall take up the expression at that point which will cause you to know that nothing has been lost—not even time. Oh glorious Blaze of Life, that looks through everything and sees the reality of being, the Now of Life and Light.

The halo is not something projected by the silly notions of vibrations, but a perfectly natural emanation of light which escapes and is visible even to the eyes of the double-minded. He wishes to fall down and worship Jesus and gets the stern rebuke "call not me good." Seeing this emanation in terms of success and joyous abandon, the human mind tries to patter it and fails—tries to destroy it by every ways and means that he can contrive—and fails. Might he as well try to destroy the light of the sun by thrusting a sword into it as to destroy the Blaze of Life which proceeds from the I AM within—the soul which has awakened to its true identity.

As light consumes darkness yet does not consume it, so the Blaze of Life consumes the darkness of human thinking, and the glorious, divine indifference to appearances from this height always brings results. The sick are healed, and the poor are fed, and the good spell (gospel) is preached without any conscious effort. What is all the worry and flurry about making the world good and getting rid of evil? You can only get rid of that which is within yourself.

Perhaps you do not like this. More than likely you are one of the consecrated ones, one of the appointed ones. But remember, *I* stood not in pulpits but in the stable and was associated with those you called harlots, winebibbers, and sinners. Remember that *I* am not any more in your holy churches, with all their rules and regulations of who and why, than I am in the lowest dive. Dare you to deny this? Then you dare to say to Me that *I* am not omnipresent. You dare to say that *I* am more present because of you and your chattering words or your idle thought about making Me appear. You shall see in good time.

I am the Blaze of Life within you—*I* give life to the dead and dying by recognizing the eternality of life. *I* am that which can again establish the Lazarus, even though to all the human reasoning it is impossible. *I* am the doer of the impossible. *I* am the one and only expresser, and *I* do not find it exciting or miraculous that My good should come into manifestation without effort. *I* am effortless, like the light breaking across the skies of night—your skies of night. Even as you read this, *I* am ready to break across your consciousness and cause you to see beyond the limitations of your human thought. *I* am the Blaze of Life.

"If ye be in the Spirit (Consciousness), ye are no more under the law." The law of what? The law of your own belief. If ye be in the Spirit, do not fall down and say it is hard to be in the Spirit. You are at this instant, and always have been, in the Spirit of life—only the holy torch which is within you was not fired into flame by pure recognition of the God-presence in everything, here and now and always.

Awake thou, across the black night of trying to make Me appear. Behold, *I* stand at the door and knock—not as some strange historical character but as a living, breathing, pulsating life, a Blaze of Life which has come finally into expression. Do you hear? You who read this page? Yea, this line? *I* am looking through your eyes; let Me illume the page for you—let Me illume life for you and cause you to see the flower before the seed and the bird before the egg.

Be still—do not attempt to blow the Blaze of Life out or make it flicker to fit your poor human capacities. You will begin now to appropriate some of the things which *I* could not tell you of back in Jerusalem. You will begin to absorb some of the good which is all about you. You will be quiet. Yes, you who read this page; your chattering will be over; you will feel My presence, and after that, nothing will matter, and all the idle trying to demonstrate Me will pass, will be lost in the Blaze of Life which will reveal to you that there is little need of demonstrating that which is present in all its fullness. You will go by the way giving, giving—giving such a precious substance that even your gaze resting upon so-called evil will transform it. The halo that will emanate from you will not make you an impossible saint of the early-day Christians, but will be the light which you will carry into the everyday world and which, as you go on your way, will fall into many a basement dwelling and make it a palace.

Again will come to your remembrance (for when you recognize the Blaze of Life, you will not be a healer but a revelator of the *isness* of the kingdom here and now) the glorious and divine indifference—divine indifference because it does not recognize the two powers, one good and the other evil, but the *oneness* of the spiritual universe, which by reason of its oneness and unity become indifferent to beliefs amassed from the judgment of appearances. Healing will flow into expression as naturally as light dispels the shadows. Why should one knowing the nature, then, of shadows not be indifferent to them—regardless of how real they may appear? He is divinely indifferent to them and knows that nothing he does or attempts to do with a shadow will change its essential nature; but recognizing the truth that with the coming of light the end of the shadow automatically takes place, he turns his attention to light.

I am the Light of this (present) world. *I* am always very near, as near as you yourself are to any condition or situation. *I* am a light which is set upon a hill, thereby illuminating all the valleys and ravines of human belief. The light piercing the dark caves of the earth reveals precious stones, unseen by the human eye unaided by the light. The Light of the I AM pierces the deep recesses of your human thought and finds hidden there royal diadems of jewels of attainment. Such jewels are beyond all price. They are there in you, awaiting the recognition of the light within.

When you identify yourself with this glorious Light of the within and are God-conscious of Its presence, then will your words shoot forth on streams of lightning and illume the way for not only you but for countless others. It will be with the impersonal and impartial giving of this Light that great effulgence will come to you; the halo shall be extended, ever taking in newer and fresher mansions in the Father's house. In the language of the Scriptures, you shall "enlarge the borders of your tent."

You cannot bring the Light as something you carry in your hands or something you force into expression by so much thinking, but you show forth the Light by reason of being the Light yourself. The whole process will become more and more unconscious, and hence, more and more natural, reliable, and productive of results. "Blessings, blessings, blessings—so many you cannot count them" will become true. So automatically will the Power of God function in your life that you will presently be swallowed up in it and be unable to sort out demonstrations of the Power and talk about them. So many blessings you cannot count them. You will not be seeking little gifts of the Spirit; you will come and lave and drink and eat.

"Eat my flesh and drink my blood" has small comfort to a helpless sinner, as taught by theology. But it is a wellspring of beauty, a gushing fountain of life and vitality, to the awakened soul who once recognizes that the flesh to be eaten is the substance of Spirit made manifest—the heavenly manna—and the blood is the inspiration of God Almighty coming into his life with a great Blaze of Light.

You who are silently reading this, do you hear what *I* say unto you? You who read—you. Be still; that which is back of all thought is a thinker, and the thought is only the farthest reaches of the impression put through the limitation of the intellect. Be still, then, and *I* will impress you with something so wonderful that it cannot be put into words. You will begin to accept some of the new proportions of the new heaven and earth. Be still—do you hear? Learn to accept your good. Leave the dry letter of the word and imbibe the soul. It is well with the Now. Do you hear?

I have strange and wondrous things to impress you with. My promises are kept—do you hear? Read, then, one of them and see for yourself. Are you afraid to trust Me wholly and alone? *I* give nothing to cowards because cowardice has narrowed down the aperture to such diminutive proportions, and only the tiniest ray can penetrate. Listen:

> Henceforth I call you not servants; for the servant knoweth not what his lord doeth; but I have called you friends; for all things that I have heard of my Father I have made known unto you (John 15:15).

Do you hear? Believest thou this? You who read this page? You? As a servant of the human beliefs, you knew not what the master or overlord of chance and fate did. But *I* call you friend and make known to you all things that *I* have heard of My Father. That is, *I* am ready to reveal to you the depths and the heights of the true Word of God, which is above all the human laws and opinions. Be still—you who read this. You.

If you give the "cup of cold water," you will not go unrewarded. If you give the glorious freshness to the perishing soul of the Presence of the God-Power here and now, and if you bring to him the kingdom of heaven as present, this will quench his thirst and moisten the parched lips, so long in the desert of human reasoning.

Seek not what you shall eat ... neither be of doubtful mind ... seek the kingdom of heaven; and all these things shall be added to you (Matt. 6:25, 33).

This is just the reverse of the strange idea that by reeling off words you can get things or that the reason Jesus came to earth was to give men a power to work magic and get prosperity and all sorts of things. Jesus came to reveal the Kingdom as here and now, where everything is already in manifestation and does not need to be recreated by a thinking man.

Be still, you who read this page—you. Do you believe that "all these things will he added unto you"? Yes or no? What can you do about it? Can you make them appear?

Blaze of Life—Blaze of Life within you who read this page—shine forth. Shine forth, dissipating the shadows of disease and inharmony. Shine forth. Shine forth in all thy splendor. Reveal the Kingdom as here and now, complete and whole.

Chapter XIX

Who Are You?

Who are you? And to what end were you born? You who read this book—to you *I* come. *I* ask you the question you read because, if you are willing, you shall see the answer written in fire over the portals of your universe. Slave! Arise from the pigsty of your prodigality and return to your Father.

You have done a deal of talking and reading, taking lessons and listening to lectures. What is the final result of all this research in the material husks of reasoning but a few grains of truth? Do you believe one percent of what you say? Why prate about the healing influence when before you opens a door of no-healing? Who are you to be healed, and of what?

Beloved, why will you wait longer for the realization of that which you have been telling of for years? When will you arise as the Son of God, the living God, and assert the freedom that awaits you?—above all treatment; above all worry and wonder; above all trying to make it so. When are you going to accept what you are saying?

"I am the Son of the living God." Do you believe this? If so, you are at this instant facing a radical change in the outward expression which will be so far above the old concept that you will stand in amazement at the glory of it all.

Just what do you believe? Is there a God, an All-God in your universe—or is the devil of your belief greater than the God who created everything? Are you still getting rid of evil? Do you still insist that evil is real and true? You say no to all this, but what do you do each morning? Do you recognize God as present and give thanks, or do you run to some person who is supposed to be ordained to speak the Word of Truth and see what *he* has to say about your problems?

When will you have the courage to jerk the curtain away from this hypocrisy and see that the "holier-than-thou" has left a home full of disease and unhappiness to come to his office to advise you how to live and be? When will you come to Me? When will you open the door and let Me in? When will you thrill with the realization of the present—the Now? Do you not see that man needs no mediator between himself and God and that nine-tenths of the mediators could not stand the searchlight of truth? Back of that hypocrisy is a temple full of moneychangers and dove sellers. Look them over! When will you awake to the sovereign truth that there is such a thing as God? How much longer will you sit with the swine and ask for that which is poured out to you in abundance?

When will you awaken to the full truth that is here and now? When will you say within the courts of your own being, "It is wonderful"? When will you recognize the God-universe and begin to live?

When will you realize that God is always present, in spite of the harpies who insist that you must have a special training to know this? When can you arise and say within your soul, "It is wonderful"?

What is wonderful? Life is wonderful when you come to Me, the I Am—that which existed before Abraham, that which is and always shall be, that which cannot be sold, preached, or put into print—that which *is.*

It is wonderful. Bless you. Fear not; *I* have led you along the path. *I* have proved to you the folly of seeking help through man; you have finally been humbled before the stable of your own true Self. Take off your shoes (human understanding); you are on holy ground. Be still, very still, and bring your gift. You have arrived at the point where you do not seek Me for a gift, but seek Me to bring a gift. You bring the self and lay it at the manger of My birth (My realization), for in reality *I* was never born and never died, and *I* am you.

Fear not. You have paid allegiance to many beautiful faces and holier-than-thou appearances. Flash the light of truth on them; say to them, "Physician, heal thyself," and see them shrink away under the excuses. When one comes to you who is divinely appointed, rest assured that he will not have to tell you this and that he will not parade his personality before you. He will not gloat over his achievements and inflate them to unbelievable heights. He will not annoy you by the tiresome and ugly description of his family.

When *I* come to you, *I* come free—untrammeled and above all the petty cares of life. I AM—do you hear? *I* have no name but the I AM. *I* am he that should come, and when *I* come, you cannot but realize that all schools, names, persons, and places are wiped out of the picture. *I* bring a new day. Do you want to give up the old day, with your past wonderful achievements? Do you want Christ? Or do you want to impress people with the trifling that you did or left undone, but that you now glorify? Are you a glutton for praise? Are you afraid that someone will not remember that you did a good deed? Who are you and what is the authority which makes your deeds so glorious?

Be still, beloved! You have passed through all these states; you have told Me ever so often of the wondrous deeds you have done. You have tried to write your name on the sands of time. You have paraded in My robes, holier-than-thou—I know you.

What matter? Beloved, *I* know you are tired. One system after another has failed. Even your desire to destroy Me has failed. *I* am and always shall be—and though you would slay Me in one inexplicable way or another, rest assured, your efforts to destroy Me are naught. Bless you.

You are tired. Why do you not let go of the prodigal and return to your Father's house?

When will you come, beloved, out into the sunshine of realization—the Presence of God-Power here and now?

Do you believe one-tenth of that which you speak? Are you a man of matter? Or Spirit? Who are you? What is the end of your appearance in this plane?

I come with light and healing in My wings, beloved. Why will you kick against the pricks? How much longer must *I* speak to you and have you turn aside? How much longer will you divide My garment among you? How much longer will you set yourself up as the holier-than-thou? When will you be the Son of God? When will you act like the Son of God? When will you dehypnotize yourself from the belief that your knowing or thinking will do anything?

"Awake thou that sleepest, and Christ shall give thee light." Do you believe anything *I* have told you? Do you think for a single moment that there is such a thing as God? If so, what is this foolish effort you put forth to bring Me into manifestation? When are you going to live to the height of your understanding?

Are you one of those who sell Me in the open marts? Do you sell My prayers for a price? Do you sell My spoken word, colored with your personality, for a salary? *I* shall finally tame you; you will finally hear Me; you will destroy yourself on the wheel of life. Do you actually believe that there is such a thing as God, or do you just imagine that? Are you selling Me for a price? What are you doing? Who are you, anyway, who parade your personality, which will soon fall into the dust—you and your little achievements? When are you going to drop off this foolishness and perceive Me as the true Father of the universe?

"Awake thou that sleepest, and Christ shall give thee light." Do you believe that? Or is it a fairytale? When will you begin to say, "It is wonderful, it is wonderful"? When will you begin to realize the Truth of Life? When will you actually say, when asked who you are, "I am the Son of the living God"? Do you think, believe, or know you were created by God? Your results will be accordingly.

Remember this: My kingdom *is*—it does not have to be explained or "put over." It *is*. All the jabbering that you are going to do will not make it more real than it is at this moment. All the pathetic ideas that you entertain about Me and My kingdom will fall away when the light of the heaven here and now appears—when your soul automatically arises to the point where it can say, "It is wonderful" and mean it.

Chapter XX

Courage

*He that hath the true fear of God in his heart hath
no room therein for any other fear.*

—*Cromwell*

As every positive word has a negative counterpart
and interpretation, so the word *fear*, which is the ghastly
hydra-headed monster that besets the footsteps of man
from cradle to grave. It has a thousand different titles and
names, is personal and impersonal. One person might
quake with it, another thrill with joy. It is easy for a trained
pilot to soar about the heavens like a glorious bird, but the
same movements may cause the untutored to be thrown
into paroxysms of terror and dismay.

So likewise the expression *fear of God* brings to the
minds of many the fear of a most terrible tribal God who
takes keen pleasure in pouncing upon them at unexpected
moments and bringing the most fiendish devices to pass,
while to another it means a reverence and security with all
attending benefits.

A savage, after seeing some of the terrible things that
can be done with electricity, might fear it and even obey its
injunctions as interpreted by a savage medicine man. He
might prefer to stay by his rushlight rather than have anything to do with this fearful thing. But an enlightened man
will not deprive himself of the glorious benefits and help
derived from the proper understanding and use of the
power. There are many people who profess to be civilized,
who smile with derision at the so called savage—and worship in ignorance a God as replete with whims, moods,
and fearful power as any heathen God dared to be. While
professing to worship a Father-God who is mindful of His

own, they are filled with superstitious beliefs concerning Him.

I heard a man talking to this God regarding the need of money, with great emotion in his voice, finally conclude his high-flown statements of an impersonal God with: "Now, Father-God, you know if it is best for me to have this money it will be forthcoming." He was the spirit of humility and contriteness and was as near a pagan praying to a glorified figure of clay as he could possibly be. Imagine praying for the invisible current of electricity to let you have light if it thought it was well for you to have light. If you are in total darkness and have to read, it is an obvious fact that you need light. Yet thousands are thinking to wheedle some special favor from this God, while afraid and filled with superstitious fears regarding Him, so that their humility is nothing but a robe of hypocrisy.

"The fear of God is the beginning of wisdom." The wisdom spoken of is the understanding of God, and the fear that is mentioned is the reverence that one naturally has for fundamental laws.

A musician, the more he awakens to the glorious realm of harmony, the more he reverences (fears) the laws of harmony. He does not see in them anything that will destroy him or from which he can curry personal favors, no matter how contrite he has been, no matter how many times he has told the principle that he is a miserable artist, full of terrible discords, and unworthy of the power to express harmony. As an artist, he knows that the moment he falls away from the laws of harmony, chaos is produced in his playing, and he will eventually completely destroy himself as a musician if he continues to disregard these laws for long.

"The wrath of God"—or electricity or discord—then must be in the keeping of man, no matter what may be said to the contrary. The wrath of God is man's own wrath, or his ignorance or "fear" of God in the negative sense of the word. Many people have interpreted the fear of God as meaning a power that constantly requires sacrifice of everything but the most ordinary things of life. Others have a tribal god who is a bestower of personal favors. Still others imagine they are one of the few chosen to express this power—that they are especially consecrated and that all others must look up to them. Jesus, the great Wayshower, seeing this tendency in man, made it clear that the power he was employing was impersonal and as available to the man in the street as it was to him. "Call not me good." Well might he have said, "Do not worship me."

"I am wonderfully and fearfully made." Do you begin to understand the *fear* of God and how it operates successfully over the "fearfully" made body? Do you begin to see what is hidden in the word *fear*? Do you understand how the currents of electricity run freely over a perfectly equipped house? Wherever there is wiring and equipment, there it appears in whatever form it is needed, and that form is to neutralize a belief in a lack of some kind. So also the "fear" of God operates over the body, which is "wonderfully and fearfully" made.

Many an electrically equipped establishment has a system of wiring and switchboards, wonderfully and fearfully made. The most ordinary man in the street would not find it anything unusual if told that the same power could freeze and burn at the same time, in the same room; he would not find it strange that this power could connect him instantly with the other end of the earth. No, he has recognized this fact and accepted it.

That the power we call God operates in the same manner is not understandable to many people. They want to know what "method" or what power you use to neutralize disease as differentiated from poverty; what affirmations you say to bring about happiness as differentiated from those used to produce prosperity—as if there were a different set of currents in an electrical wave to produce different manifestations. God is impersonal, omnipotent, and omniscient, as well as omnipresent. He is everything at the same time. The moment you recognize the Presence of God in any place, the situation or condition of human ignorance becomes nil.

When you begin to recognize the impersonal nature of God, great areas of fear leave you. You realize then that it is not a matter of the power working or not—it is a question: are you willing to let it into manifestation? When you are ready, *I* will do the work. When you are ready to stop this ridiculous praying to a man-god and come before the Presence, with the glorious readiness to *let* the Power into expression, then will you see and know: "The words I (the I AM) speak are not of myself, but him that sent me." The "words" are the manifestations that you give forth as the *Son of the living God.*

Do you begin to see why it is that if you "make your bed in hell" (the hell of belief) *I* am there? To recognize this is to see the darkness of hell dissipated in the light of Spirit. To the human sense, flames may have light and a burning heat, but this is nothing as compared with the light of Spirit. Hell is always personal and limited to the belief of a person; heaven is universal and everywhere present and is available to everyone.

That this power has always been goes without saying, just as we know the principle of the automobile has always existed. Jesus might just as well have ridden into Jerusalem in an automobile as on an ass, as far as the existence of the principle is concerned. No one recognized the principle; hence, it did not seem to exist. In the same way, you, in your human darkness, do not recognize the presence of heaven here and now, and so it does not exist to you.

Because of the limitations of human language, terms of symbology and parables are used to bring out the hidden meaning of the visible-invisible; yet it is ridiculous to compare the power of God with the power of electricity.

The Power is so much beyond the limited illustrations man can give that words utterly fail to convey the idea, and the best illustrations only raise many queries in the mind of the reader. Who can define the Infinite?

The first fear, then, to be eradicated is the false interpretation of "the fear of God," not the belief in a power opposed to God. When you are unafraid of God because you are beginning to understand the All-Now of the All-Presence and are ceasing the terrible struggle to make this Power work according to human standards; when you cease to fear Him as a terrible tyrant, meting out horrible punishments to helpless victims of his caprice, then will you begin to know "the peace that passeth all understanding," for "in the twinkling of an eye," you will see that all fears are induced merely by the lack of understanding of God—"the fear of God." The understanding of this great Power so completely fills you that there is no room for any other "fear."

"The fear of God is the beginning of wisdom." The reverence for, and aligning of oneself with, this glorious Power is the beginning of wisdom. You will see the human fears for what they are—the product of a double mind.

A man I met, working in the service of God, was afraid lest he could not get sufficient money to keep his church in operation. What about it? Do you suppose this great Power, desiring to express Itself, fails to supply everything necessary to make this possible without the aid or assistance of man? Who is this man who thinks he has to strain every nerve to bring in the Christ-kingdom? Who is this poor benighted soul who imagines that if he does not make a place for God to express, God will not be expressed?

Where is that one who is seeking no favors or any permission to express that which God hath given him to express? Where is the one that needs no recommendation but finds the temple doors flung wide open to him? Is it that one who, as Cromwell says, "hath the true fear of God in his heart" to such an extent that there is no room for any other fear?

You who read this page, what is the nature of your fear? First, what of the fear of God? What do you actually feel in your heart regarding this God? Are you afraid of Him? Do you fear Him in the old sense of the word, or do you "fear" (reverence) him as the great impersonal Power? If you but learn to be unafraid of this Power, you will be like the learned electrician. Your fear and superstition regarding the truth will melt away, along with the other fears of evil, poverty, and disease.

The fear of God is the beginning of wisdom. Do you hear, you who read this line? The door is opening to you— the door into the glorious land of understanding, through which you may enter and be free. They (your fears) may seem terrible and imminent. They may seem sure to annihilate you until you learn that through the unafraid state of mind they will flee. You cannot fear anything when your heart is full of the fear of the Lord, remembering that you are wonderfully and "fearfully" made and that the power which is to activate this mechanism is now in full manifestation.

"Come, ye children, hearken unto me; I will teach you the fear of the Lord." The I AM will reveal to the unafraid soul all the wonders that are hidden beneath the "fear." The eyes of the blind will be opened. You will begin to see that although some may say, "Peace, peace, and there is no peace" and some may retain "the fear of the Lord" in their hearts and suffer the pangs of the damned, yet others may be so filled with the "fear of the Lord" that no other fear can enter.

Do you see? Do you hear—you who read this line? Does not your heart suddenly burn with a glorious joy? Are you not aflame with the glory of the new revelation— you who read this line? You have nothing to fear because you have "the fear of God."

You will begin to read the secret doctrine and see the things that are hidden away from the wise and prudent. You will begin to see how the letter often contradicts itself as well as confuses. Witness this for prosperity:

> By humility and fear of the Lord are riches and honor and life.

Interpret this from the negative meaning of the word *fear*, and you have a contrary argument to the non-fear state that appears to be necessary for the relative world of finance today. Fear is to be ejected at all costs, and as *fear*, so it is. But consider this with its true meaning, with your heart full of it, and you will see that prosperity is not a matter of demonstration, but a matter of recognition. You cannot help but manifest prosperity any more than an electric bulb could refuse to illuminate when the power is turned on.

"Search the scriptures." You will learn to search the deep, hidden meaning of the Word. *I* will reveal Myself to you.

It is only when your heart is full of the *fear* of the Lord that you can truly say, "I shall fear no evil," concluding with the glorious reason: "For thou (the understanding) art with me."

> He that hath the true fear of God in his heart hath no room for any other fear. It is wonderful.

Chapter XXI

O Colorful One

I am the Great White Light in which all the visible and invisible color of the universe and heaven rest. My name is O Colorful One. *I* am full of light that is white and glistening and at the same time is multicolored and many-hued. My white light passes through the prism of human thinking, reasoning, or teaching and takes on seven distinct rays, and man, looking through a glass, darkly, and with the double eye, sees as many different paths all claiming to be the truth. But so long as a man remains in the personal idea of the truth he has not yet seen the Great White Light of his true Self, in which are hidden all things—hidden only to the eye that is double.

He may follow a single ray of color, thinking that he at last has the truth, only to find that it terminates in disillusionment. One by one, he may exhaust the paths, until finally he comes to the Great White Light of his Soul. It is the whole garment alone that can satisfy, and this comes not by a mediator but through the Christ within. Until man learns this, he will go seeking in every strange place and chasing every will-o'-the-wisp of color, hoping to find peace and the All. He will find what the man finds who believes literally that a pot of gold hangs at the end of the rainbow.

Pretty soon he begins to see the Great White Light of his Soul, and as he recognizes this, he sees hidden in this all the glorious colors of Soul. A million colors and tints burst upon his startled eyes as he goes from glory to glory, for he suddenly realizes that for the first time he is seeing. "Having eyes, ye see not" is changed to the glorious explanation "whereas I was blind, now I see."

He is thrilled with the exquisite bliss of the awakening in the new heaven (state of consciousness) and the new earth (manifestation in the flesh). He finds there everything he has tried for long years to demonstrate by one means or another. He finds there overflowing abundance of the All, and he is unafraid and naked. There is nothing between him and the truth—he is lost in the great swirl of color, of light and glory. He is bathed in its golden mists. His feet are lovely upon the mountains of inspiration and along the still waters, limpid and blue. He lies upon the breast of the new earth under the shifting gold dust of the sun of life.

He tastes of the bliss of the peace which passeth all understanding. He is suddenly One with the Universe, with the All. He is everything and nothing at the same time. "When a man loses his life, he shall find it"—when your personal sense of trying to run the universe is ended and you are willing to let go of the petty personal desires, you shall taste of a fruit of life that will again admit you into the portals of your lost Eden.

Ah, how fair it stands, and has always stood, awaiting the one who could lay aside his dusty, worn, travel clothes and put on the white, shimmering robes of the Son of the living God. "Eyes have not seen, ears have not heard, neither has it entered into the heart of man the glories prepared for them that love thy law." What you are about to experience when you can give up or let go of this tinsel personality—painted with the colors of effort and struggle to be or do something personal—is so far beyond anything that has ever been written or told you that the comparison is absurd. What you lose when you give up or let go of the personal something is the difference between Jesus and the Christ. And this giving up is not a straining thing when once you understand the truth as taught by the Master.

Gladys Smith may have been the teacher's pet, been called a pretty child, and been the pride of her family, but Mary Pickford absorbed all of this Gladys Smith and expanded to a creature beloved by thousands. She pushed out the border of her tent beyond anything little Gladys would ever have dreamed. Do not be afraid that your darling—the little personality that has perhaps to your eyes attained such wonderful things and wants credit for it always—is going to be lost by giving up and letting the Christ into expression. You will lose nothing but the prison of a name and a following, and find a Name and a Following a million times greater than the little consecrated soul you thought you were when working to bring in the millennium and save the world.

He who travels alone travels far—no man along the way can discuss these things with you. Either you do or you do not know that within you lies this great fountain of life which gushes up into a pure white stream—shoots far up into the azure skies and is transformed into a mist of glorious color by the Sun of Life.

You are this fountain of pure White Light which is everything and anything. It can be that which it will and is so chameleon-like that it can harmonize with its surroundings either for protection, lost to the human eye, or to bring forth a glorious revelation. The great floods of understanding will ever be able to speak in that color that is understandable to the listening one. Thou art all colors, twinkling, blazing, flaring up into expression.

O Colorful One, the soul of me, only through this great at-one-ment can I ever find the satisfaction of life. Only when the impersonal comes to be the personal can I repossess my universe and find it heaven here and now.

Many have whitewashed themselves over with a false humility and set themselves in the highways of the world, proclaiming in all their meekness that they are the consecrated souls and have come to save the world from sin. They have come to save nothing, not even themselves; they are merely selling My robe, casting lots for it in the open market of life—drawing their white garments away from Me and making themselves official stone casters. Do not imagine that any personal teaching, however high, will satisfy you—nothing but the discovery of the Great Soul of your true Self will do that.

"Let the filthy be filthy still." Let the personal teaching remain personal; you will find your soul in due time. A filthy mind is always seeing filth. A nude statue made to represent the truth is to him something obscene and dirty. Find out what a man is condemning, and you have a concrete picture of that man. You give yourself away when you criticize another; you are only letting the wise man see your self, which is hiding behind a personality.

O Colorful One—the soul of you is that which makes you to know concretely, right here and now:

> I am the light of the world (your manifest world); he that followeth me shall not walk in darkness (human beliefs), but shall have the light of life.

The I AM, the O Colorful One, will cause you to see the impossibility of walking longer in the human beliefs and limitations of life. Many things that you formerly consigned to the "yes-they-may-be-possible-when-I-get-the-understanding" will be natural. *I* have things to show you that *I* cannot tell you.

Dominion, dominion, dominion—not domination. This is what *I* give you. There is no need to dominate in the kingdom of heaven, for that is only bondage. What you dominate occupies your whole time and attention, and hence dominates you indirectly. *I* give you dominion, for you have the cloak of invisibility, the cloak of many colors, any color. Do you understand, O Colorful One?

Yes, your soul leaps with joy with the boundless possibilities of the Sons of the living God—with the serene joy of the expression anywhere, and at any time, in the manner necessary. Not just a painter or a lecturer or a dancer, but an O Colorful One, who knoweth the deep things and can give to every man that which he asketh—not as a personal gift, but by way of Self-revelation.

I am a pool of iridescent flame. In Me is all; without Me is nothing. When you are lost in My will, then you automatically function from the heights of bliss, abandon, and expression. Your individuality is not lost; it is found. The deep springs of unknown talent and accomplishment gush forth into expression. You shall speak with new tongues, both literally and figuratively. You shall be at that instant just exactly what you recognize yourself to be—when you do not strain to recognize it but just *are* it by recognition and assumption—very easy, as the color of white broken up into the rainbow melts from one to another hue.

O Colorful One is the soul of you. It plays into expression as the light plays on the water—there is no resistance to the light. It does not need to combat its supposed enemy, the darkness. It finds nothing there to fight. So the human mind, when lifted to the understanding of the Son of the living God, will find that what it formerly considered obstacles will disappear. What to Jesus was a problem was nothing to the Christ; what to you as a human personality may seem an impossible, insurmountable obstacle is nothing to the soul of you. The tiny resources which you hugged to yourself as a personality become as a drop in the bucket compared to the overflowing of the windows that are opened in heaven when you recognize the Power of the Son of the living God.

Saul, going to his duty of fighting sin and evil, is blinded by the white light—so white that the human eye has not yet perceived it. It would blind the human eye because of its limited capacities and because of the indescribable colors and hues. Millions of tints and nuances are revealed, but by this very blinding is the obstruction removed, the name changed, and the way opened—the new way.

All this is just in front of you—you who read this page. Do you hear? You? When will you lay aside the trinkets you borrowed from your masters in Egypt? They have served you well, but they are also souvenirs of your bondage.

The letter that you study is merely a memory of your bondage to the human concept of truth. Presently you shall cast that aside and exclaim in the soul rapture of the Son of God, the O Colorful One: "I am free born. I am a Son of the living God. I am a joint-heir with Christ.

Glory, glory, glory—and a flood of white light, with its billion of colors and tints, shall descend upon you. Your eyes shall be open, and you will know that "it is well" and that nothing matters but you and your soul. And in finding this out, then for the first time and in the true sense of the word, everything matters and is your special charge, and the command, "Feed my sheep" will be literally understood and not mutilated into a personal service.

I said "feed my sheep"—not destroy my sheep with the personal fears and personal teaching. Who are you?— standing there with that great mantle of personality about you, passing out some tabloid statements of how to get things and how to attain spirituality by following after you. He that setteth himself up shall be abased. Remembering that the Master had no patience with hypocrites, have a care that you be not classified with those who were called vipers. To whom will you be Judas? You may be running about smartly correcting others and thinking thereby to win a special reward. Watch!

O Colorful One, the soul of you will cause the mantle of secrecy to envelop you. You will not care to chatter about the findings of truth—they will be too precious. Once you have been shown the jewel, the pearl of great price, and seen the luminous floods of color of your real Self, then you will know that nothing matters but the following of your own soul instructions. How and whither, no man knoweth. He that hath many cares must remain with the household of the human thought and try to set it in order—and at the same time, he may be a doorkeeper and have many duties to perform.

Do not think, because you discover your true Self, that you will sit idly by and pass out wisdom on a golden platter. You will live and release wisdom on rays of light that the whole world will see. Fear not! If there is anything to you, your fame will find its wings. The dogs barked at the feet of the Master as he passed through the streets of Jerusalem—the holier-than-thou dogs and those who would have destroyed him. Fear not: *I* am mightier than any combination of human belief. Those that are for thee are greater than those beliefs that are against thee.

O Colorful One, soul of me, shine forth—that is, the word shine forth in the particular nuance of expression that is necessary at this instance to bring out the glories of heaven on earth. Can you see how heretofore you have asked for nothing, for you have not known how to ask? You have asked for some trifling thing in order that the human self might be glorified—in order that you might gild over a human personality and make the world fall down and worship you. But now you ask in the true way, that of appropriation. Can *I* speak plainer than:

> Ask, believing, ye receive.
> Before ye ask, *I* will answer.

Am *I* then, the soul of you, a liar? Is My word broken constantly and not fulfilled? Do you hear? You who read this page? You? Do not ask another—ask yourself. What are you afraid of? Letting go? Letting Me direct your way? Are you going to bend it in order that it may suit another's idea of you or what another thinks you should do and accomplish? Be still! Until you can get over that, you can never know peace.

Come out from among them (human thoughts) and be free. A man's enemies are those of his own household (consciousness). These are the only enemies you have, and yet you have a world full of them because you see your human thought reflected in a million mirrors of the universe. What hope is there for you to change the reflection in the mirror? *I* said, "*I* am a new creature in Christ Jesus." *I* call to your attention over and over this statement, for finally you will hear it—a new creature has no need of the old appliances, bandages, and appurtenances—fears. Do you hear? You who read this page—right now? You?

The open road lies before you, no matter if you are bound head and foot with human beliefs. *I* say unto you— *I*, the O Colorful One, the soul of you—*I* say to you, to you who read this page, to *you*: are you listening (feeling)? *I* say to you, "Rise up and walk."

Do you hear? You? *I* am speaking to you from out the depths of your very being. *I* am speaking to you from out the fount of life. *I* am telling you something that is already possible, awaiting acceptance, awaiting recognition. The open road lies before you, the road upon which all things are discovered, not created. It is the Way of Life, and it leads all over My Universe and goes directly to its robe and ring and upper chamber, and finds its purse and scrip.

Do you hear? *I* am that Way, the Blaze of Life, the O Colorful One. *I* go before the human manifestation and see that the way he travels is clear and that there shall be no stones for him to stub his toe against. Are you afraid? *I* shall clothe thee in the many-colored, seamless robes of pure white which shall be all things to all men.

"Be ye transformed by the renewing of your mind." *I* did not say you should be patched up and fixed up to look better and to have more of My goods. I said *be*—now, here, at this instant—*be* ye transformed, not temporarily changed—glistening, shimmering, shining, white and all colors at the same time. It is wonderful, wonderful, wonderful. Heaven and earth are full of thee—of thee, of thee—the All-inclusive, the One of which you are a point in consciousness. All My glorious Self pours through you into expression, and yet all of it is left. No amount of hearers can ever exhaust music. Because a person listens to music, he does not destroy anything of its volume, and yet he has it all. So will it be with you.

So will you go into your own garden and find the eternal Christmas tree, the gift tree, the tree of life, situated beside the inexhaustible river of life, and you shall be at peace. It is wonderful, O Colorful One; it is glorious.

You who read, do you hear? Be quiet then; let go and see the salvation of your true Self pour out into expression. Even as *I* now pour out the words to you on this page, so will *I* pour out to you your true and wondrous expression.

It is well. You shall descend into the cleansing pool of life and there taste the bliss of heaven.

It is well with you—the mist-ifications of the earth beliefs are even at this instant becoming more translucent and clear; "then through a glass, darkly" is beginning to become "then face to face."

O glorious, O Colorful One with healing in your wings, with the strength that is beyond all human limitations in your arms, with the glory of youth eternal written all over you, you are even now stooping down to the human belief and lifting up the poor little personality, until it shall be swallowed up in the million hues of spiritual wonders of the Kingdom here and now.

Chapter XXII

B.C. and B.J.

Attention is called to the fact that there is no such period as B.C. (Before Christ), for the simple reason that "Before Abraham was, I am." The Christ has always existed, and there is no date before that, for it is before the human, relative sense of time existed. There is, as has been brought to light, B.J. (Before Jesus), which gives us a date some two thousand years ago.

So is it with you, the real you, the Christ of God. The Son of the living God does not come under the relativity of time, for there never was a beginning or ending to the birthless, ageless, deathless Christ in you, whose measure of time is eternity and is therefore above all the ravages of time and the dangers ensuing therefrom.

Your Jesus, John Smith, or whatever you call yourself, has only existed for a limited number of years. It has gone through the experiences of the Master in varying degrees and has been crucified. It is the only thing that could be crucified. The Christ of you could never be pierced, nailed to a tree, slandered, maligned, or hurt; this is only possible of Jesus, and for this reason the Master saw the fallacy of trying to do anything from the Jesus state of mind. It was a constant fight from cradle to tomb, hence, his discovery and priceless gift of wisdom to the universe! "I (Jesus) of myself can do nothing ..." but knowing that the Jesus was but the shadow of the soul and realizing that to become prodigal was to suffer all the limitations of the belief, he advised against considering the Jesus. He counseled the student to go within, saying "If I (the I AM) be lifted up (to at-one-ment with the All), then I shall draw all men (man-ifestation) unto me."

Do not call Me good, speaking of Jesus with the limitations of a belief man—a man of certain strength, of certain health, of certain limited earning capacity. Many people are today sitting in the seats of the scornful, calling the world to view their intense spirituality, shouting from the housetops, "Come and look at my wonderful power and view my elegant family. We are all workers for the Lord; we are the only ordained ones; come to us for spirituality; all others are liars and cheats." It is as though the Master had never lived and given to the world the simplicity of the Kingdom here and now.

"You deny Me"—you deny the statements of Christ because you cannot see them. Your eyes are holden because they are loaded with the blindness of your John Smith. You deny Me; you read My words that the kingdom of heaven is at hand and straightaway make Me out a liar by trying to prove that the world is full of evil which you, a special one, are sent to destroy. "I do not come to destroy but to fulfill." *I*, and the I AM of you, do not come to destroy; It comes to fulfill—fill full everything that is empty. Every vessel in the human consciousness of your Jesus is poured full to overflowing with the substance of the Christ-Mind, and you are found not wanting in anything.

It seems too good to be true that the kingdom of heaven is here and now and that it cannot be brought into visibility by long sermons of so-called holy people. No man can bring in your kingdom of heaven. It rests with you whether you will continue to make Jesus a liar or a truth-sayer—whether you believe that his saying "The kingdom of heaven is at hand" is the truth or a lie. You take this magnificent wisdom and extract a grain of truth; perhaps you have to run to someone else to find out what he believes about it and get turned awry by personal teaching, teaching crammed full of personality.

It is quite easy to understand the limitations of Jesus. He was of lowly birth, no breeding, no special talent, no education, no money. "Is not this the carpenter's son?" What good can come out of a dirty little town in Judea? These are the questions which immediately beset the personality and to which the personality, or Jesus, must answer, "I am Jesus; I am a carpenter; my parents are poor; I have no education; I had no chance; my earning capacity is that of a day laborer." Whereupon Jesus is assigned to his proper place in the human category.

What hope is there for you, as you stand today? The soul of you may burn with an ardor too intense for words, yet because you keep on admitting and recognizing yourself as John Smith, you go under the limitation of that personality. It is only very occasionally that you perceive the light, and at such times you exclaim with great joy, "I have had a demonstration." You have had a demonstration of the Christ of you, which should be in constant manifestation. Presently you will tire of the great desert spaces between demonstrations and arrive at a place where you will open the door to the real you and see every limitation of the personality broken.

The Master showed clearly that, while Jesus could only be a carpenter, the Christ (which he explained was common to every man) could transcend with natural ease every limitation to which the Jesus was subject. In other words, he found it true that "if ye be in the Spirit, ye are no more under the law"—that is, if you identify yourself with the I AM, the Christ-consciousness, not as something unusual or something to be used against evil but as your real true Self which is above the beliefs of the limited Jesus, you will begin to function on a plane of attainment, a place of fulfillment. It is not the overcomer; it is that which comes over. The more unconsciously the processes of life become the more perfect they are; hence, the difference between the baby crawling on the floor and a man flying through the air. He has come through all the stages and has forgotten them, having taken not the letter or labor of it all but the wisdom which lay there. The reason a baby can finally learn to walk is that it has the ability always there, awaiting recognition. The moment it is recognized, it either accepts it or fails to see it as a possibility.

This is the order of the human education—that a man must study years and years to be able to lecture and teach; yet we find the man Jesus, through his understanding of the Christ, lecturing in the temple before the wise and learned. How could this possibly be? He had no training. You belong to one or the other of two classes: "you say it is four months"—"I say, look again." A chorus of voices protests with the usual "Yes but …" and they must wait for the four months. But the other one will thrust in the sickle, for the word is, "The fields are white now," not at some other time.

When the inspiration says, "You do not need to think what you will say—open your mouth and *I* will supply the words," who are you, with your human intellect, to go against the magnificent truth. Even though you may have all the degrees that mankind can bestow upon you, who are you to dare to deny Me, the I AM, and try to impose the foolish wisdom that you have been prating for years, and your stupid arguments that you have amassed from the human appearances? Either you can accept the inspired word of Christ, or you are going to argue. If you argue, it is because you have never heard. Either God can do it, or it cannot be done—and neither you nor ten thousand of your kind, with a million proofs of the human belief, can offset one letter of the truth.

"Yes, but that was Jesus" is one of the old sayings, one of the old arguments to excuse ourselves from getting rid of the human personality, with its limitations and beliefs. Jesus said, in speaking of the Christ-Mind, which, I repeat, is common to every man: "The works that I do ye shall do also, and even greater works than these shall ye do." Is this a lie? You have to answer that for yourself. When you can, you will also see that the veil is rent and that all that is left is for you to make a clear decision as to whether or not you are willing and ready to be born again.

If you want the Christ only as a demonstrating power, so that you may stand and make long speeches about what a wonderful power you have and recount all the wonders that you have done, then you will have little of it. If you want it because you see the glorious realm of the Sons of the living God, then the doors will burst asunder, and you will know that nothing which has gone before matters. You will be instantly freed into the limitless sea of substance. You will hear the command and obey. "Come, eat and drink without money and without price." The password for attainment is yours, simply for the recognition of this Christ within, as *you*.

Some will stand and wait for a sign. No sign shall be given; you have already had the sign—I AM, and *I* am in My heaven right here and now; *I* will make the hell that John Smith is in, no matter however involved, melt away right before your eyes, both literally and figuratively, into the effulgence and radiance of the kingdom of heaven. "Oh, taste and see."

Beloved, the words are true, and you will see that all this straining to do the works of God has passed away into the place of actually expressing the power without effort. Effortlessly it comes into expression; at that point to decree a thing is to see it into manifestation. *Who are you?* And to what end were you born? Do you think life is meant to be a constant fight, a constant study or dead letter? Will it ever mean to you the here and the now of what your soul knows to be true?

We see further this exemplar Jesus, weighing average weight, walking on the water—an utter impossibility. We see him setting aside the human laws of weather. How could a carpenter do either of these? It is interesting to note these from the actual and figurative points of view. Spirit has no weight; hence, it is heavier than nothing. Weight belongs to the human reasoning, which it constantly overturns. Not so long ago they insisted that a body heavier than water would sink, but a piece of iron or steel—in fact, a mass of steel much heavier than water—is made to float in the shape of a ship, and nothing is thought of it. Hence, one by one the old beliefs give way. That which at one time is said to be impossible becomes reasonable when it has to be accepted, and it is incorporated into the beliefs.

When you recognize that Now, in the golden Here, you are the Son of the living God, you will hear the clatter of the scaffolding of human beliefs and teachings crashing to the ground in order that the New Idea, the perfect Mansion, can be made visible. We have mistaken ourselves; we have failed to let go of the scaffolding, and the glorious Christ-man is still hidden under the letter of the human teaching. We have even tried our best to make this scaffolding look like the Christ, doctored and treated it and tried in every way to better it. "You must decrease, I must increase" is the law. The human personality, the Jesus of John Smith, decreases by being lifted up to the recognition of its true Self, and it is then said of you, "How does this man speak with such wisdom, seeing he has no learning?" You find the way, for *I* am the way, and *I* have a way that ye (the human reasoning) know nothing of.

A serenity comes to you, a "peace that passeth all," a glory of rest which belongs to the Sons of God; not inactivity, but a joyous rest from all the struggle and strife to please a tyrant, a God of likes and dislikes, a God that you have set up for yourself, which you have chopped out of a tree and fashioned with gold and tinsel and then fallen down and feared.

You shall come out into the place of attainment—not attainment for worldly show but the secret attainment. You shall pass a man on the highway and, by speaking to him silently or openly, shall heal him, and he shall know you as a nameless being, the Christ, instead of lauding a personal name to the skies. You shall go your way, for the doors of the universe shall be open to you. "I (the Christ) go before you (John Smith) and make straight the way." Do you hear? You, I mean *you*, who at this instant are reading these lines. I said *I* (the inner Lord—your inner Lord) go before you and make straight the way. Believest thou this? Surely not from the appearances. The sick body, the depleted vitality, and empty purse, all are symbols of that to which human limitations can come.

Be still! If you cannot accept the truth, be still; do not argue. If you cannot hear Me as *I* speak to you *now*, then open My holy book, any book, and let Me speak to you. The time will come when you will hear My voice because you will recognize that it is the only voice possible for the Christ-Mind to hear. The jabbering of doctrines as "mine and thine"—the puffed-up personalities who make it a business to cast stones and screech from the pulpits "God is love" (that is, if you see it exactly as I do)—shall be naught but the distant chirping of so many insects as against the roar of the thunder in the heavens. You hear because you believe it is possible for the Son of God (You) to hear—and only because of that.

"Who did hinder you?"

"Well, one person told me one thing and another told me something else, and I was confused."

If you have been confused by the avalanche of teaching of the Christ, why do you continue to seek among the husks any longer? Why do you not cease from the classrooms of the human mind and enter into the courts of the Lord? You and you alone will be the one to rise and go to your Father. No matter what you know about it, until you *believe* the inspired word as possible here and now, you will never see or hear it. You may catch fleeting glimpses of it, but you will not know the joy of living, moving, and having your being in the All-God—the freedom of the

Sons of God, the joy of Eternity, the Being that does not date Itself, but is and always *is*.

Chapter XXIII

The Mechanics

When you come to the place of recognition—and by that I mean when you have actually accepted the fact that the universe is under the direct control of a Power designated as God, or Life, and not subject to the limiting laws of evil belief—then you will see that before the chicken or egg, before the flower or seed, is a power which conceived the thing in its totality.

The supposed evolution from the invisible to the visible is only the sluggish action of the human thought, trying to account for everything through the elements of time and space. An idea does not have to be worked out in the universal Mind. As in the single grain of wheat lies the substance which eventually sustains a whole army of people, by a somewhat slow process of growth, so wrapped up in every idea is not only the means of expression itself, but the complete expression in its entirety.

It is by looking at a single grain of wheat—putting it through the limiting processes of human estimation and then pitting the findings against the power of consumption of the army of people—that man comes to a full stop and says that it cannot be done, or that if it be possible, there is such a great time lag which intervenes between the single grain of wheat and the thousands of loaves of bread necessary to sustain the mob, that it is hopeless to expect anything from that source.

This may be true and reasonable from the limited human concept; it is merely used as an illustration of comparative sizes. An idea as small, symbolically speaking, as the grain of wheat has within it the substance sufficient to fill the greatest cavity of human belief—not by a slow process of evolution from the invisible to the visible, but by sudden recognition of the allness everywhere. How it will come into manifestation is not known to man—"not even the Son, but the Father knoweth."

The Son of you in this respect might be judging from appearances and in a manner waiting for something to take place—might be speculating on how it could take place. The Master, recognizing this, knew that if the Son conceived the thing as complete and finished and rested in it, the mechanics of how it would appear would take care of themselves, and the idea would have within it the means of bringing itself into full expression. "Take no thought" is the command—after having laid carefully before the mind the fact that taking thought could not add one cubit to one's stature and asking the pungent question: "If ye cannot do that which is least by taking thought, why do you try to change the eternal ideas?"

Man is beginning to see that all the thought in the world is not going to change the eternal laws of the universe. Nothing shall be added to, and nothing taken away from, that which is All and in all.

By this sensing of the eternal facts of the universe, the feeling of perfection and completeness of the idea in its entirety becomes a constant experience. Out of the chaos of the night of belief, in the blackest mire of human thought, man conceives light, and suddenly the darkness is absorbed; it has disappeared, and the experience not only seems to have been a dream, but actually *has* been a dream, a semi-conscious state. The experiencing of any evil is but a semi-conscious state. Man is conscious of some action, but his interpretation, through his belief in evil, causes him to experience what is termed evil.

"It is well," if conceived as a reality, will set everything right in your universe. How? I know not—I am not concerned. It is so. "Believest thou this?" It cannot be reasoned out; all the human intellect in the world cannot explain how you can be prospered yet have no increase of symbols or things but the use of the invisible substance of the All. The unseen substance is part of that which "eye hath not seen," but it is there, and man senses it. It is not necessary for him to have an outward sign; he finds that he has in reality experienced the use of substance—done things, gone to places, expressed himself—and actually his bank account has not had more symbols of dollars and cents.

So he finds eventually that his acceptance is pushed to a point of accomplishment. "Only speak the word." A word of itself would do nothing. "Peace, peace, and there is no peace" is a fine illustration of what the empty word may accomplish. The living Word, the Word of God, is not clothed in any language. A hundred men, all speaking different languages, would understand the living Word, whereas merely hearing the different noises made by one another to represent what the Word is would be a veritable tower of Babel.

Come, awake! A new day dawns, so far removed from the trying to make things happen by jabbering words at God. What have all the words accomplished? How often have you pleaded with God—begged, beseeched, beaten at the gates of heaven—and been turned away empty? Thousands are waiting in the desert for drink that you alone can supply through the new plane of recognition. You can give only that which they have already, as it might be said that Jesus gave life to Lazarus by calling his attention to the eternity of life.

"And man became a living soul." Everything into which the breath of the living Word is breathed becomes a living manifestation of God. Breathing the breath of life into a man-ifestation is only another way of stating the power of recognition. It is a far cry from the glorious truth "Ye shall decree a thing and it shall come to pass" to the "How to have prosperity, health, and success" by rattling off a lot of words in tempo or out of tempo. "Prove me, and see if I shall not open windows in heaven and pour out a blessing ye cannot receive." You will see that the *Me* is the Christ within your consciousness that is to be proven and that the windows of heaven must also be in your consciousness, for heaven is a state of consciousness—a state of Self-expression or revelation. The blessing that is to descend to the Jesus is then directly out of the consciousness of Christ—not in some far-off locality, not something that has to be made to appear out of the skies or through some strange treatment.

Prove it you cannot, until you become fully convinced of the Presence of the Power of God, Life, everywhere—complete and whole, merely waiting recognition. Then the ideas containing in themselves the complete expression will, to what the human sense appears, evolve into manifestation. But the whole thing—the how, why, when, and where—is in the *now* and is done at the instant the recognition is made. Man has nothing further to do with the proposition but to lend himself as an instrument, a willing instrument, to bring about the manifestation through the beliefs of time and space. There is, therefore, no concern about the outcome; it is sure and certain and has not one chance of not appearing, for in reality it is already there, invisible to the double eye but plainly visible to the single eye of the I AM.

"Believest thou this?" Do you think it possible with this God-Power, or will you still interpose a lot of traditional ideas and things that you have gained from going up and down and to and fro in the universe of changing, shifting belief? Yes or no? Either you do or do not; no middle ground is possible. All or nothing. God is and is All, or you have two powers. What is the good of trying to fence with the idea any longer? If your eye is double to evil and good, then you cannot expect to experience the power of the Christ. Evil seems more real than good to most people because they actually have accepted it as so, although they emphatically deny it. The least thing that happens to them they exclaim, "Just my luck!" Not that the exclaiming of this means anything; it is the accepted power back of it.

The mere words would mean nothing to a Frenchman; in fact, a whole string of negative words would mean nothing to him unless they were in French. We must get back of the symbol. A gramophone record has no power in its word any more than the praying machines used in the Orient. Be still. Stop trying to tell Me what to do—stop trying to arrange the outcome of things. Be still ... be still. Accept the unspeakable Word of life which shapes in your mind as "It is well," and lend yourself, a wholly willing servant, to perform the mechanics, if any be necessary, to bring this idea into manifestation.

Do you hear? You who read? God is—you are—it is well. Get that woven into the fiber of your mind, and glorious melodies, complete symphonies, will be played across the strings of your heart. You will become so busy appropriating the glories of heaven here and now that you will neither have time nor need of demonstrating the power—it will be a continuous manifestation of one glory after another. "From glory to glory," from revelation to revelation, not in the impractical, intangible, emotional way, but actually "the Word made flesh"—the actual manifestation in daily life. You will be found walking in the garden, your garden, gathering fruits and flowers where you will. Not as a special favor for a few moments, after which you are to be turned out again in the desert of human experiences, but as an heir, an owner, one who appropriates that which is.

Came Jesus and stated the nothingness of time and space. "A thousand years is as a day" and vice versa. "Instantly he was on the other side," disappeared when in crowds. Dare you to think on these things? Not as a glutton who would consume the food in order to show his size; not as one who wishes personal power; but as one who travels alone into his own kingdom of Self-expression and finds it normal and natural, as well as convenient, to be possessed of these powers.

Be still. If *I* could not tell you everything in Jerusalem because you could not bear it, *I* shall not always withhold it from the ears of those who are ready and who have washed their robes clean from all this self-seeking and this attempting to shout "Look at me—I am holier than thou, let me show you my bag of metaphysical tricks." Come away! Be still! Leave your nets. You cannot catch many fish, anyway, until you know that the substance is there in its entirety and you have only to accept it to find the nets breaking with manifestation. Not for show, beloved, not for talk—do you hear? Be still ... be still ... be still. It is well; fear not. Everything is all right. Do you hear? You who read this page? This word *now*? You?

In the twinkling of an eye it is done—so quick that the flurried human thought has no time to flash an answer. So overpowered and bowled over is his reasoning that he exclaims, "A miracle—some supernatural power at work." What difference what he calls it or how he tries to explain it? He has to admit that it made itself manifest not through his best accepted chain of laws, but in spite of them, and that those best and finest laws he has conceived for himself have been completely ignored.

Why will you examine into the human laws to find out whether it is possible for Me to express? Fold up your tent and steal silently away from the noise and clatter. *I* have something to say to you alone. *I* have something to show you, something to make your heart so full that it shall run over into the whole universe. It is wonderful! Do you hear? You who read? You?

You make and break all human law; it has no basis. A traffic law in one town may be broken in the next while fulfilling the laws of that city. It is nothing but a human limitation. If it were an absolute law, it would be the same forever, and breaking it would automatically produce results. This is true of all the laws of sickness, poverty, and evil. Be still—*I* have much to say to you. When you are ready and willing, *I* will perform the works in such a beautiful, easy manner—even now as *I* write this book, even now as you read this page.

Even as you now hold the finished manifestation in your hands, so *I* hold it finished and complete in consciousness and am going through the mechanics of belief to bring it into manifestation and to bring it into your hands. Do you begin to see? Do you begin to read between the lines, the message that *I* cannot put on the lines because of the limitations of belief? Be still ... be still. It is so. It is well with you *now*.

Chapter XXIV

Gleanings

Let there be light, and there was light.

This was before the creation of the material symbol of light—the sun. It is just this Light that man is today seeking again, having caught glimpses of it in the instantaneous manifestation of Power, which is termed by many the supernatural power but which is in reality the *only* Power. Just as the light which preceded the sun is the only Light, the coming of this Light makes the light of high noon as twilight.

In this closing chapter, I have massed together the words of Father Divine, the leaven which, if buried in the meal of your human consciousness, will make the whole mass leaven. One of Father's songs:

> Behold, *I* stand at the door of your heart and knock. *I* am the fount of every joy. *I* am all intellect; you don't have to grope.
>
> *I* am all success. *I* am all health. *I* am all wealth. *I* am all strength. *I* am all intelligence. *I* am all wisdom. *I* am all knowledge. *I* am all love.
>
> *I* am all that you can desire, and *I* am knocking at the door of your heart. Every time a man seeks joy, it is *I,* knocking at the door of his heart. Open unto Me. Open wide. Let Me in.
>
> Speak Lord, and thy servant heareth. *I* speak, and My servants will hear, wherever they are. *I* do not ask them to hear or demand them to hear. *I* speak the word and they hear. *I* bid them see and they see. *I* bid them walk and they walk. *I* bid them be prosperous and they are prosperous.

In speaking of human relationship, Father Divine said:

> You cannot have mothers and fathers, sisters and brothers, relatives and family, etc., and have Me too. You cannot rob God. Someone is nearer and dearer to

you than *I* am, and then you wonder why *I* do not claim you. That is why you cannot get to Me. That is why you are subject to sickness and trouble, because mortals are subject to those things and you are living in mortal consciousness.

God declared, "Let there be no division among you." Every distinction and every division is a curse to the nation. Jesus, in the seventh chapter of St. John, prayed to make them One, even as we are One. Some of you claim to have been in the Truth for years, and yet you have sisters and brothers, mothers and fathers, husbands and wives, etc. Such of you are separating yourselves from the Infinite Whole and joining yourselves to the individual world.

The Sonship degree of spirit prayed the Father to make them One as we are One, and that is what I have done. I have put you all in a melting pot and have made you One. Now, that is the way back home, where the Christ is. It is the only way back home—denouncing these mortal things and then renouncing them for Christ.

In speaking about the new life, the new idea, in relation to its former bondage: "That which is born of flesh is flesh, and that which is born of spirit is spirit." The new creature, then, does not go back and converse with old relative conditions if he expects to take on his new heritage:

I have come to take you *out* of the grave, out of mothers and fathers, sisters and brothers, husbands and wives, children and parents, races and creeds, out of mortality into immortality. I have said nothing of how long you have been dead or how long you have been in this state. Lazarus had been in the tomb four days, typifying a time equal to the four thousand years since Adam, and people thought he was dead, saying, "He stinketh."

People have thought the seed of Christ in man is dead, it has lain so long, but it is not dead, and I have proved it is not dead, and I have come to awaken you. You are going back to the Garden of Eden as you were before the fall. If you will live in accordance with My will, this automatic machine within—the Christ—will begin to work in you, if you abide in this consciousness.

When the new idea is born, it must of necessity have a new abode:

I'm taking your mind out of the imaginary heaven, for as John saw, in Revelation, twenty-first chapter, the first heaven and the first earth have passed away. I'm canceling the imaginary heaven and earth out of your consciousness. That's what I came for, to erase that imaginary heaven and earth from your mind and prove to you that the kingdom has come and the will is being done.

You have prayed that the kingdom should come. How can it come when you have the imaginary heaven in the way? Get it out of the way, and then the new heaven and the new earth can come in. The first heaven and the first earth shall not be called to mind anymore, and I am getting it out of the way so that the new heaven and the new earth can come in.

We have heaven here because we are making earth a paradise. The old seed idea was all right, but this is the harvest now. The old idea that was planted in your consciousness for years is bearing fruit now. The prayers of your dear mother, the prayers of your dear father, have been answered, and the new heaven and the new earth have come down from God out of heaven.

In speaking of the reason for so much sickness and failure among those in metaphysics, Father Divine says:

I was just considering how slight a thing it takes to recognize the body, the actual body, of Christ. It is wonderful! Truly wonderful that it is that way. I repeat again that quotation I so often use: "For this cause many are sickly among you, because they do not discern the body of Christ."

It is truly necessary to discern the actual materialization of the Christ in order to be freed from mortal limitations and be saved. The Truth teachers, and the Truth students particularly, have discerned the spiritual Christ, but they have denied the materialized Christ. Consequently they are subject to all kinds of sickness and trouble in their physical bodies because they have not included them in the Christ. They say the spiritualized Christ is perfect in them and is not dependent upon a physical body. Then why bother with the physical body? Let it go down into the grave. But Jesus came to save physical bodies, and I am here, the materialized Christ, to save your physical bodies.

By gazing upon this perfect manifestation of the materialized Christ, you will reproduce the same in your own bodies in every joint, every sinew, and every bone. You will see good in your hands and fingers, in the fine skin, etc. You will feel this boundless joy coursing through you. Limitless blessings! He who is an antichrist must be half-brother to the atheist. The antichrist does not believe in the materialized Christ of nineteen hundred years ago, or of today. The atheist does not believe in God. Take these things in, dear ones, for your consideration.

Speaking of the impersonal nature of the Christ:

Though *I* should not be visible to you, *I* am always with you. *I* have established this Truth, and with or without a body, it is operative. It is even more operative when you do not see Me. Nothing can stop the operation of this Truth, for *I* have established It. If America should sink and every visible expression were to sink in an earthquake, it could not stop It. If you are sick, all you need to do is call on My name, and you do not have to see anybody or anything.

Explaining the manner in which manifestations were concreted, or brought into visibility, Father Divine said:

That which you think is spirit, that which you think is only mental, can be materialized by the power of Christ Itself. "As many as received him, to them gave he power to become the Sons of God," etc.

When you believe in the materialization of Christ, that gives you the power to materialize things, but the average person, who believes only in the spiritualization of the Christ, cannot materialize things. I might say here, if I can coin a word out of nothing, they can only "imaginationize" things. When you realize that "the Word was made flesh," then you materialize and bring out the activity of Christ in you. When you come to this relation, things are actually materialized. Humanity

169

has lost sight of the great importance of the materialized Christ. For your highest good, it is necessary to realize that Christ has been made flesh and dwells among us.

Dear ones, I am sure that those that are in Truth have been taught that God is a Spirit; they have misconceived the idea that the Word has been made flesh. Many make shipwreck of good faith and cause themselves to be atheistically inclined and have caused many more to be atheists than deists. Every spirit that confesses that Jesus Christ is of God is of My kingdom, but every Spirit that denies that Jesus Christ has come in the flesh is an antichrist. He is separating his body from the Spirit.

God declared: what *I* have joined together "let no man put asunder." How dare you separate Jesus from Christ or Christ from Jesus. If you do, you are separating your body from the Spirit, and "whatever you measure shall be measured to you again, and it shall be full, pressed down, shaken together and running over."

Again I say, "Your ways are not my ways, saith the Lord, for as the heavens are above the earth, so are my ways higher than your ways."

Now realize, dear ones, that it is for your good to see the materialization of the Christ. Until the Word was made flesh, we could not behold his glory, "the glory as of the only begotten of the Father, full of grace and truth." But not until it was made flesh could man behold all the glory of God. Since you beheld His glory, therefore "of His fullness have all we received, and grace for grace."

Do you not see that step by step it came into actuality as we grew in the knowledge of the Truth? Then of *all of His fullness* have we received, grace for grace. Then you, as well as I, will be the identical duplication of the Christ that was manifested nineteen hundred years ago.

Excerpts

"Do I give absent treatments? No, because God is present everywhere."

In response to the question of how to go into the silence, Father Divine answered that it was unnecessary to sit and go into the silence if you lived in the silence. By silence, he meant silence of mortal opinions and beliefs.

"Beloved, now we are the Sons of God—God in any individual expression of Himself. The manifested Christ reveals what the unmanifested Christ conceals."

"He will come as a thief in the night—that is, unknown to you, and masked or disguised."

"Since Christ came, you have had the same right to the tree of life that Adam had before he sinned."

Father Divine refers to the Lord's Prayer as having already been answered. We need a fuller recognition of this fact, to consider it under the light of "Before they ask, I will answer." The important part of the prayer is: "For thine is the kingdom, and the power, and the glory, forever."

"Paul said, 'For of the fullness of his glory have we received, grace for grace'—all of His glory, every bit of it. We have received *all*—so claim your right and press your claim."

" 'He restoreth my soul.' Your soul was once stored up in God before Adam and protected by Him, but it has become scattered and is now being gathered up into Him. 'He restoreth my soul ... my cup runneth over. Surely goodness and mercy shall abide with me all the days of my life: and I will dwell in the house of the Lord forever.' I *know* the Christ in Me can save you. I *know* it—if you will *let* the Christ in you save you."

"The Spirit of the Consciousness of the Presence of God is the source of all supply and will satisfy every good desire. That is the way I get my money, and in no other way. The abundance of the fullness of the Consciousness of Good—no place is vacant from the *fullness* thereof. *No* space is vacant. No space in you is vacant. It is in every joint, every sinew, every vein, every bone, and every fiber and cell of your body—the *abundance* of the fullness of the Consciousness of Good. I am speaking to every cell in your body, and the Christ in every cell is responding and coming forth to the Christ."

"And it is done here and now. If you will abide in Me, and let My word abide in you, you will, through constant praise and thanksgiving, create such an atmosphere about you that your message, silent or spoken, will continue to bless and heal and draw all joy and health and love and life unto you."

"It is not necessary that one come to Me as a person to be abundantly blessed, but that they form a mental and spiritual contact, raising their consciousness to contact the Christ-Consciousness, if they would be even as *I* am, free from all bonds and limitations. The Spirit of the Consciousness of the Presence of God is the source of all supply and will satisfy every good desire."

One of the "angels" at Father's asked this terse question: "Would a chick hatched in an incubator call the incubator its mother and look to it for its inheritance?" The answer is obvious.

"It is essential that all moral intellect be stilled, that the voice of God may be heard. A complete relaxation of the conscious mentality is absolutely necessary, being still and knowing the I AM God within—speaking, sacrificing, and laying down every prop that tends to hurt or bind, and depending solely on God alone. Then running with patience the race, for it is not unto the swift and the mighty, but unto him that endureth unto the end."

Postscript

Beloved—at this instant, as you read, we are in the glorious silence of the Presence. The Father within and the Father without is present. We are pausing in the flooding light of Truth, which is permeating the entire universe. The heart fills full and runs over with the joy of this Presence. The former things have passed away—you are entering the new Kingdom. In this hushed and lovely moment of silence, we give thanks to the Father.

Son of the living God, arise and shine, for thy light has come. The new day has dawned, and the shadows of the day of relativity are fleeing before this Light.

Michael Pupin once said:

> These big stars are only the beginning of God's creative energy. The human soul, insofar as science can penetrate, is the last chapter of cosmic history as far as it has been written. It is in the soul that Divinity resides. When we think of that, we are not so small. Science has found nothing in the universe which even compares in importance with the life of man.

It is, then, to Father Divine that I give thanks and praise for having shown me something of this wondrous Life which looks out from the stars instead of up to them.

"Blessings, blessings, blessings, so many you cannot count them." Praise God, from whom all blessings flow. You are laved in the glorious flood of Life—it is well, and so it is. Selah.

FINIS

About the Author

Walter Lanyon was highly respected as a spiritual teacher of Truth. He traveled and lectured to capacity crowds all over the world, basing his lectures, as he said, "solely on the revelation of Jesus Christ."

At one point, he underwent a profound spiritual awakening, in which he felt "plain dumb with the wonder of the revelation." This enlightening experience "was enough to change everything in my life and open the doors of the heaven that Jesus spoke of as here and now. I know what it was. I lost my personality; it fell off of me like an old rag. It just wasn't the same anymore."

His prolific writings continue to be sought out for their timeless message, put forth in a simple, direct manner, and they have much to offer serious spiritual seekers.

Walter Clemow Lanyon was born in the U.S. on October 27, 1887, and he passed away in California on July 4, 1967.

Made in the USA
Las Vegas, NV
04 September 2021